# *The Beginning of the Beginning*

*An Artist's Journey On Creativity*

By Claudia P. Gray

**Lotus Life Publishing, LLC**

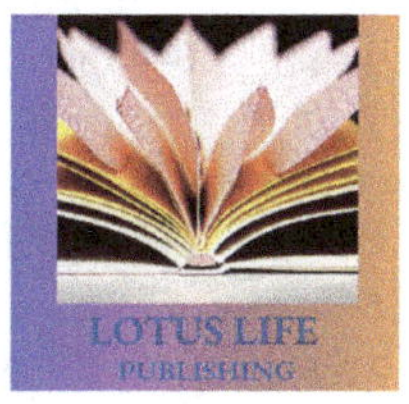

The Beginning of the Beginning
An Artist's Journey on Creativity



Lotus Life Publishing, LLC
Atascadero, California, USA
First Edition
Published 2023



Kindle ISBN: 979-8-9883058-0-4

Paperback ISBN: 979-8-9883058-1-1

Cover design by: Claudia P. Gray
Library of Congress Control Number: 2023908327

Printed in the United States of America

# CONTENTS

# LIST OF FIGURES

# INTRODUCTION

Creativity is an illusive and complicated activity which many artists and philosophers have attempted to define. This was originally written as a book manuscript for my Masters Degree Capstone Project including my personal exploration of creativity and its development, in my mind, and in my ten year practice as a professional artist. Throughout my time as an artist, a personal creative theory has been forming along my journey. Mindfulness, art, photography, slumping, glass art, paintings, spiritual and philosophical concepts are explored. Master artists, such as, Ansel Adams, Cindy Sherman, Georgia O'Keefe and Claude Monet play special parts my inspiration. At its current junction of writing this book, my personal creation philosophy can be summed up accordingly: creativity results from emotional expression and self preservation. This book is meant to not only define and explain creativity, but to also inspire others to create.

Of Special Note: Because this work was created originally as a research thesis on creativity, at the time, MLA formatting was utilized. In order to preserve its essence, the MLA style was kept for this publication.

# DEDICATION

I heartfully dedicate this project to my four children,

Olivia Gray
Tommy Gray, Jr.
Alexandra Gray
Jack Gray

I feel so blessed to be your mother. I remember with such fond memories all the different art projects, home studios, and activities we have shared. Currently, with some of you, we still joyfully collaborate and create together. It has been a true pleasure seeing you all grow and flourish into the fine people you have become. In a way, parenting is also a creative endeavor, and in that context, you are all my greatest co-creations yet. I am grateful for all the lessons we learned together as you are all wonderful students, as well as teachers. Thank you, also, for all your support, feedback and time you have given to me as a mother, as well as an artist. I love and cherish each and every one of you for the unique beings you are.

# ACKNOWLEDGEMENTS

I would like to acknowledge the many people that helped me get to where I am now on this creative journey. First, I would like to acknowledge Nuncia and Tony Agosta, my parents, who had courage to immigrate to the United States of America for a better future for their family. Without their journey, I would not be where I am today. A special acknowledgement to my dear sister, Roxana Greenman, who was my first best friend and has given me so much love, laughs, and support throughout our lifetime together.

A special note of thanks to all of my art teachers, and especially Sama Wareh who gave me my first show and believed in me from the very beginning. Much heartfelt thanks to my many spiritual teachers and artists friends who gave me the encouragement and opportunities to learn things that I never thought were possible. To Dr. Barbara Wright and Eva Hodjera, much love and Metta to you both for being my "Aunties," and leading the meditation group where I learned more about Buddhism and met such wonderful people and inspiring artists. Your group was essential for my various personal development and especially for both of my art and Buddhist paths. To my clients, friends, gallery management, and art show promoters, too many to name here, that each gave me special mental gifts and take-aways that I have somehow incorporated into my art.

I feel much gratitude for my Masters Degree professors at Tiffin University that helped me not only grow my formal training, but inspired and challenged me to stretch my mind and perceptions of art and philosophy. Thank you, thank you, thank you… dear Professors Jessica Doyle, Dyrk

Ashton, Matthew Pearcy, Gregory Downing, Vincent Moore, Jessica Gilpatrick, and Stavroula Kalogeras.

Lastly, I must also acknowledge the great artists that inspired me to no end and continue to do so, Claude Monet, Cindy Sherman, Georgia O'Keeffe and Ansel Adams. How could I ever let you know how much your own art meant to me as I grew and how it still puts a smile on my face.

# CHAPTER 1: INTRODUCTION - A CREATIVE JOURNEY

What is creativity and how does it start? Why is there a need in the artist to make form out of nothing? Why do we make stuff, and is there a process that takes place? Now that I have been a professional artist since 2012, and at the time of writing this book in 2022, currently finishing a Masters program that has me studying philosophy, humanities, film and art, I am wondering even more: what is this creative urge about and how does it start? In reflecting about what makes one creative and what that has meant for me. I can perhaps start out with my Artist Statement and take you on my creative journey of the beginning of the beginning.

Part of the statement includes that I know that my creativity was always there, perhaps hidden from my active self, but it still remained in the background growing and developing. Ever since I was young, it seems that I have always had a real need to be creative. Whether, picking up watercolor over thirty years ago, remodeling kitchens, redecorating homes, creating gardens, writing professionally or currently trying new Mixed Media techniques, I have always had a need to have my creativity come out in one way or another.

If I had to pinpoint my process, the central theme has always been, take something or a location, re-work it and make it beautiful. In the beginning of my artistic journey, it seemed like I wanted to improve on a form that was already there. At some point around 2012, I started working with glass and I ventured into ecofriendly glass art. I was still satisfying the desire to reincarnate something that was on its way out. In this case, they were glass bottles being recycled or thrown in the landfill. During those years, I took the bottles and melted them into their next lives: slumped bottle cheese trays, sculptures, ornaments or sun catchers, or jewelry pieces.

But what exactly drives what I do and what is it the core of this need to be creative? One thing that might come into play is that I am deeply inspired by nature and Eastern Philosophy. There is a correlation between my art and the universal processes. For instance, when I work with paint, I am reminded that everything is fluid. When I work with molten glass, I am reminded of fire and impermanence. When I take photography in nature, time stops and I am aware of the present, capturing and freezing a moment in time. When I work with a blank piece of tile, I am enthusiastic about how the design and colors I choose will change its blank slate appearance. There is no doubt creating art gives me a sense of peace, harmony, and a big smile (see fig. 1).

So does this art that I create need validation from external forces? After it is created, does the creative process stop? Does the audience continue the creative flow? I believe this is the case sometimes. For example, feedback could be considered an extension of the original artistic intent. In my case, when people see my work, I would like them to be honest, whether they resonate with it or not. My philosophy, is that I can always take something away from how each person perceives and interprets my art. I don't necessarily need the feedback once the piece is finished, however I do welcome differing perspectives and interpretations. My life's philosophy is that I am here to learn and I am constantly

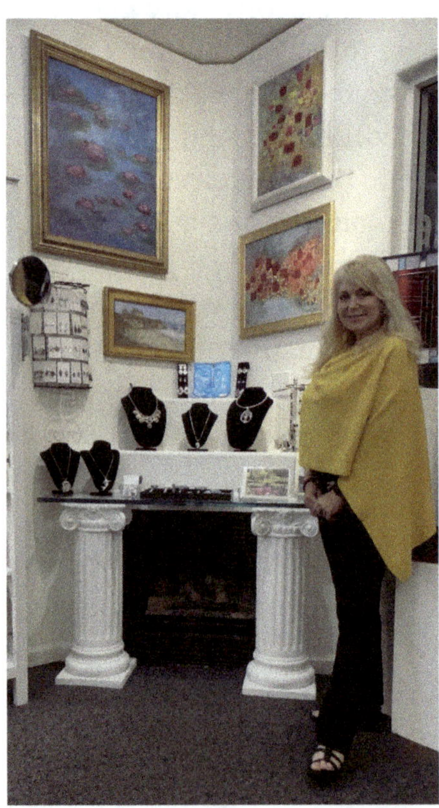

Fig. 1. March 2022 Gallery Exhibition for my featured artwork including glass, paintings and jewelry. Claudia Gray. *Self Portrait: Happy Artist*. 2022,

evolving from each piece or technique that I use. Hence, other people's opinions are another educational tool that I utilize. However, I don't necessarily need it or ask for it. Albeit, if it is freely given, then I do listen and take in what the person is explaining.

Assessments for a piece that is under construction is a little different. It is then, when I am still working on the artwork, that I may seek out feedback and soundboards for my ideas and techniques. I have a trusted forum, mostly my older kids and friends that I involve, if they are available to provide their thoughts. I actively listen, inquire and in the end, I may or may not incorporate their observations. Many times, the dialogue is useful for spring forming onto a more refined way of creating. With this newfound information, the artwork continues its development stages.

I have found feedback creates perspectives to my art that I may not have had if I was alone in my own little creative universe. I believe that many of my pieces have improved depth and layers because of the inspirations I have obtained by talking about the piece while creating it.

One of the things I have always wanted to do was to attain a graduate degree. After raising my children, I decided to go back to school and obtain a Masters in Humanities with an Art and Visual Media emphasis. This degree would not only be a life's dream being realized, but it would also educate me formally to matters of art, film, aesthetics, photography, literature, and teaching. Due to the COVID-19 pandemic, I decided to enter an online program. I was skeptical as to how much I would get out of the virtual format, but I was quickly surprised at the quality and quantity of information that was entering my brain. There was heavy emphasis on writing, and after many decades of not producing professional writing, I was pleasantly surprised that my writing muscles reactivated.

I did not know that studying humanities would afford me an education in philosophy, creativity, and the process of creating. This was a new thing for me as beforehand, I just created and made something, or so I thought. After some of my classes, I was intrigued to know new ways of thinking about art and its formation. I was also calmed by the fact that many times I was already intuitively doing what some great philosophers had been talking about.

It was through the study of these philosophers that I realized that I was actually an artist. Specifically, that I tend to think more like an artist, than let's say an engineer. That I also formulated, on my own, ways of creating from beginning to end, something out of nothing many times over. I, now, understand that many before me in history had shared such journeys, thought processes and techniques. Consequently, somewhere along those classes was when I started to actually feel like an artist. It is sometimes astonishing to me, that with all my experience, I still did not have my own intrinsic and internal labeling of "artist" although I had a lot of exposure in the public. For instance, as of April 2022, I have received more than ten art awards, selected as Artist of the Month on four different occasions, exhibited in more than seventy two juried gallery exhibits, participated in over one hundred juried art and craft shows, curated one gallery show, currently represented by two galleries on an on-going basis, and my glass art and jewelry have sold in over thirty-five stores in five states during a ten year span (see fig. 2).

My art was featured on the radio and several websites for advertisements, and I was even the main guest on a TV show about design where I was the guest speaker covering my art and process. Throughout this time, I was still figuring

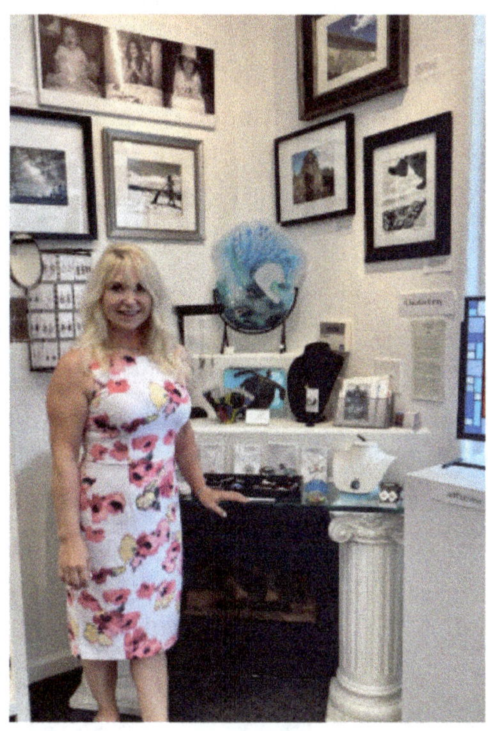

Fig. 2. June 2021, Mixed Media show featuring my work at a gallery. Claudia Gray. *Mixed Media Art Show*. 2021, collection of the artist.

out my creative philosophy and if this was just a long phase of me playing with art. Perhaps at times, I even felt like I "pretended" to be an artist. I probably had those feelings mostly because I knew I was self taught and did not have formal training. And, so I continued, with or without bouts of imposter syndrome on my mind.

Yet, I continued to exhibit and develop my talents by trying new techniques and being enrolled in art classes, continuing education college classes, and hands-on workshops. I could see and feel that I was evolving. But I must admit, that the "aha" moment of true acceptance of me being a creative entity was during one of my masters classes when we were covering aesthetic philosophies. What we studied were ideals that I already comprehended, and already lived by for decades. I then understood that I was a true artist, not just because of what I produced or exhibited. Nor was it because people validated my work with an award ribbon. It was so because of HOW I THOUGHT, processed information, and more specifically had a real need to create form out of nothing with the desire to use self expression.

All these ideals were circulating in my mind for two years. I was fascinated by the way creativity is developed and produced. This creation process of making form out of nothing, is what people call the clean slate, the blank canvas. So how does it get filled and painted? What makes an artist inspired to fill it? What materials and techniques will they use? And most importantly, what message is being communicated and WHY do they want to do it anyway? In my formal art studies, I have been immensely grateful to study aesthetic philosophers. In reading their ideals, I have had to reflect on my own creative philosophy in the marketplace as well as in my studio. Through the study of creativity and how it develops, I have refined my artistic viewpoints, my own identity as an artist and creative being.

One thing was becoming clear, sometimes creative people think differently than linear thinkers. I truly believe that one breed is not better than the other. And the world actually needs both types of minds. Nevertheless, I am more aligned with the creative flow folks than the linear types. And this revelation became a source of validation. I have actually thought this way for most of my life without understanding that I did.

As I researched many philosophers, it was clear that there is an abundance of creativity and aesthetic mysteries these philosophers attempt to articulate, comprehend and teach. It seemed that some philosophers were from years past, and others had clear explanations of how creativity works that I could easily understand. Robin George Collingwood's philosophical creative teachings were one of the best aligned with my own thoughts.

Various philosophers and some of their amazing ideas have a special place in my own creative journey. Hopefully, some will resonate with you and others may challenge the way you think just like they did with me. Certainly, it is impossible to include all great philosophers, so I apologize for not including perhaps one of your personal favorites, but I feel the ones I have written about give a general sense and an overall summary of the philosophies at play with creativity and aesthetics.

Robin George Collingwood was a professor at The University of Oxford. He wrote a 1938 book entitled, *The Principles of Art,* which highlights the philosophy of art. Collingwood thought artworks are simply an expression of feelings. Furthermore, he said that that artists possess a social responsibility which may include, articulating, clarifying, and showing emotions in the community.

In reflecting on this ideal, I can most certainly concur with my life story as being a creative type. For instance, when people find out I am an artist, I am at times seen differently. It is this holding an artist in a special gaze that Collingwood discusses. Society at times hold that artists live life with more freedom and experience things richer, with more fun, as oftentimes being categorized as free spirits. There were times that I have been given these labels just because of my profession. Albeit at times, this perception is true as my lifestyle does not completely align with the status quo nor corporate America.

Martin Heidegger, a celebrated German philosopher tackled defining beauty. He surmised that beauty is a universal concept. Heidegger, a professor at the University of Freiburg lived from 1889 until 1976. Interestingly, Heidegger aligned himself with the German Nazi movement, hence his political views were considered questionable. Nevertheless, his aesthetic philosophy are still considered significant to today. One of his ideals dealt with art helping truth to develop. In order to explain this ideal, he used the German word, *ursprung,* which translates to "primal leap." Heidegger explained the beginning of artwork is in the origin of the artists and preservers of the artwork. To illustrate this point, Heidegger used the Greek temples and how the society valued artwork. He stated through demonstrative art, the population is uplifted in ordinary life, and develops reflection for the depth of being.

Personally, I do agree with Martin Heidegger on his statement of art uplifting people as a whole. I know that my own mood positively elevates upon gazing at a beautiful or thought-provoking piece of artwork. As an artist, I have witnessed numerous times where my own art has made people happy. Not only are there joyful emotions for the viewer, but as I create art there are my own feelings of pleasure, gratefulness, satisfaction and being in a zen zone, where time is lost. Although the essence of beauty is subjective in nature, there is a universal component to it, such as, a flower or a smile which is mood altering as Heidegger stated.

John Dewey lived from 1859 until 1952 and his greatest aesthetic philosophy is titled, *Art as Experience.* Dewey articulated like art, humans value materials and nature's energy to develop life. He thought that by saying art, for example, confirms that man can mindfully renew the union of actions, needs, and sensations. Awareness and other similar items may assist with the selection and many facets of the creation flow. Moreover, Dewey expounds that art and its associations are mans' elite successes. Dewey gives meaning to practical art, such as, fine art. Furthermore, Dewey believes artists exist more happily as they create which then affords the category of "fine" art. Consequently, he includes the completeness of living in perception and creation. Contrastingly, if the artwork is not used, Dewey believes it is considered irrelevant.

Dewey summarizes non-aesthetic art as a byproduct of unhappy situations of consumption and/or production. Personally, although I concur that Dewey's arguments are detailed and fascinating, I am not in agreement with all of his ideals. As an example, contrary to Dewey, I do believe that even an artisan makes work in an unhappy state, it is still categorized as art. Furthermore, many artists create in unbalanced state, such as, most of Van Gogh's artwork was made while he was in the mental hospital, however his paintings are considered works of "fine art" and masterful. Although considered mentally ill, he poured his soul into his work and received something for the act of painting. This is evident in these two famous Van Gogh quotes, "I am seeking. I am striving. I am in it with all my heart" (ArtProMotivate.com) and "The only time I feel alive is when I'm painting" (ArtProMotivate.com).

Another form of creativity is music. Music is a part of aesthetics. Mo Di (Mo Ti), Mozi (Mo-tzu) or "Master Mo" has many ideas that are intriguing. Mozi was a philosopher and lived a long time ago. Some historians think he lived from the late fifth to early fourth centuries B.C.E., (403-221 B.C.E.), but no-one knows for sure. Mozi did not like music because of the oppression in ancient China against the class system of that time. The *Internet Encyclopedia of Philosophy* website contributors write:

> Some scholars speculate that Mozi and the Mohists probably came from a lower social class than, for instance, the Confucians, but the evidence is inconclusive and at best suggestive. Nevertheless, if the conjecture is true, it could well explain the often repetitive and artless style in which much of the *Mozi* is composed and the anti-aristocratic stance of much Mohist doctrine, as well as why the Mohists paid such attention to the basic economic livelihood of the common people. (Mozi)

In reflection, I am aligned with his desire to champion the oppressed and admonish music. One needs to understand that during the time he lived the rich folks played while the poor people paid. During Mozi's era, the wealthy enjoyed elaborate and fancy musical parties while the poor people ended paying heavy financial taxes for those events.

Clive Bell's 1914 book titled, *Art*, discusses his ideals with respect to aesthetic emotion theory. Bell writes that the item's aesthetic qualities are actually the object's evoking a feeling related to the item. Bell states the start of the aesthetics systems is when there is an experience of an emotion. Consequently, items evoking a feeling are considered as "art." Additionally, the arising of a feeling happens as the aesthetic item helps with the induction of the emotion. He asserts that in those cases the item is termed artworks. Bell explained the feeling achieved is an aesthetic emotion. Bell writes:

> All works of visual art have some common quality, or when we speak of 'works of art' we gibber. There must be some one quality without which a work of art cannot exist, which is significant form. In each, lines and colours combined in a particular way, certain forms and relations of forms, stir our aesthetic

> emotions. It will be said that the objects that provoke this emotion vary with each individual, and that therefore a system of aesthetics can have no objective validity. However, we have no other means of recognizing a work of art than our feeling for it. (Bell)

Bell also explains that the object may not be labeled art if there is no emotional reactivity for it. Thereby, unless it creates feelings, there is no essential quality to the piece. Bell states, "All systems of aesthetics must be based on personal experience-that is to say, they must be subjective" (Bell). Upon further contemplation of his ideals, I found it interesting he surmised something cannot be labeled as art if there is no emotions generated from it. Clive Bell elaborates this reflection, "All systems of aesthetics must be based on personal experience-that is to say, they must be subjective" (Bell).

I found his philosophies were worth contemplating further. For instance, if something evokes a feeling, then it may be categorized as art. Albeit, these are subjective grey lines, and who determines if a feeling is being generated? For example, if an individual derives an emotion from the object, but another viewer does not, then under his ideals, is it still labeled art? Due to this paradox, I cannot wholly agree with Bell. I hold that the item is still art, even if all people or none of the people emote a feeling. In my opinion, they are mutually exclusive. However, I will say that if a particular artwork is not capable of inducing any feeling from anyone, it is still considered art, but maybe really bad artwork.

Interestingly, sometimes I think that the artist is the one emoting and expressing ultimately putting those emotions in some form somehow, like a painting or a photograph. Pablo Picasso had a similar idea when he said, "The artist is a receptacle for emotions that come from all over the place:

from the sky, from the earth, from a scrap of paper, from a passing shape, from a spider's web" (ArtProMotivate.com). Paul Cezanne discusses feelings as well in his quote, "A work of art which did not begin in emotion is not art" (ArtProMotivate.com).

Lev Tolstoy (also known as Lyof Nikolayevich Tolstoi) is from Russia and lived from 1828 until 1910. Tolstoy wrote many books gaining the praises of Russian literary critics. One of his books, *What Is Art?,* discussed his ideal that art is a way of communicating emotion, with creating mutual comprehension as the end goal. Tolstoy explained that by understanding each other's feelings, we can successfully incorporate empathy. Ultimately, this produces a collective well-being. Tolstoy writes, "To evoke in oneself a feeling one has once experienced, and having evoked it in oneself, then, by means of movements, lines, colors, sounds, or forms expressed in words, so to transmit that feeling that others may experience the same feeling—this is the activity of art" (Tolstoy).

Personally, I think Tolstoy's concepts are thought-provoking. I can see what he is saying and I loved that he used different artists' artwork as samples to further explain his definition of art. Tolstoy depicts beauty as something giving pleasure or existing objectively in universal law. Tolstoy explains that beauty has a subjective definition, consequently he states that art is also subjective. He also expounds the moral ideals are part of the true meaning of art. I do think this is a bit dangerous, as who gets to determine what is not moral or moral in art? Nonetheless, does that ideal consider if art is determined as good, it's moral, but then the opposite would be bad art is then labeled as not moral?

There truly is no wrong or right when deciphering complex subjects as aesthetics, art and beauty. Each of them can be held on their own and individually are worth exploring and studying. There are many philosophers around the world, such as, Tolstoy, Collingwood, Bell, Mozi, Heidegger, and Dewey that have taken time and effort to define the ideals embodying artwork, creation and beauty. In my view, not of these gentlemen have been able to wholly provide complete definitions of these concepts that has been universally accepted. By its own nature, it is impossible to achieve with these subjective concepts. However, we can listen, read and contemplate these issues all the while comparing them to our own ideals. The philosophers all seem to provide a few pieces to the aesthetic puzzle, and with each piece obtained, the whole picture becomes clearer.

In summary, it is evident that around the globe, in history and in present times, philosophers have grappled with obtaining a definition of the intricacies of aesthetics, art and design. Through my studies, I learned to question their formal ideals all the while refining my own theories. Along my journey, I feel I am more in tuned with my own creative flow and the major aesthetic philosophies.

Additionally, with understanding other viewpoints, a big picture emerges. I have a better foundation as I create, analyze artworks and study philosophies. Even philosopher giant, Aristotle believes what happens internally with art is of the utmost significance. He states, "The aim of art is to represent not the outward appearance of things, but inward significance" (ArtProMotivate.com). And so, perhaps as we study more and create more, we can further develop ourselves, our philosophies and our art, just as Eugene Delacroix says, "What moves men of genius, or rather what inspires their work, is not new ideas, but their obsession with the idea that what has already been said is still not enough" (ArtProMotivate.com).

# CHAPTER 2: WHAT EXACTLY IS CREATIVITY?

As I learned more about the philosophy of creativity, I began to see that there is a flow, a divergence from mundane thinking. For instance, there has to be an inspiration, that then the person not only receives it, but then turns it into form by taking action. There seems to be so many different forms of creativity but what exactly is creativity? How do we define it? Is it measurable? Is it innate or can we cultivate it? Is it biological, psychological or both? And, are all people creative, or do artists and musicians only have it? In order to answer these difficult questions, I will start by defining the word. The contributors of the *Encyclopedia Britannica* define creativity as, "The ability to make or otherwise bring into existence something new, whether a new solution to a problem, a new method or device, or a new artistic object or form" (Brittanica).

Creativity has many facets including, originality, value, pleasure, flow, process, and imagination. Albert Einstein has described it as, "Creativity is the intelligence having fun" (Johnson). Moreover, it is considered subjective, and so the definition can be different for each person. A scientist may use the definition to study creativity and "puts those components together to say that creativity is an ability to produce something that is both novel (or original) and has utility (is valuable to someone)" (Cavdarkbasha). With this meaning, it lets scientists develop testable questions and hypotheses about how creativity stems from the brain.

With creativity, there is a process that allows problems be solved with innovation and even out of the box. Creativity seems to require that one have an open and receptive mind, otherwise the status quo would continue. Dorothy Parker, an American poet, writer, and witty critic states, "Creativity is a wild mind and a disciplined eye" (Johnson). Having an open mind stretches our perceptions, and broadens our perspectives and may even assist overcoming prejudices. For instance, a great example of innovation and creativity is when Apple came up with the iPod, which ended up changing how the world interacted with music. Obviously, we can all agree that when a painter paints a beautiful painting, that is a form of creativity. But what about other creations that are outside of the art world. Are they creative as well? Aren't we all creative in one way or another?

There is a common understanding that all of us are gifted in our own unique way. Albert Einstein has said, "Creativity is seeing what everyone else has seen, and thinking what no one else has thought" (Johnson). Some people are just a little more open and receptive to different ideas. Creativity in a way, is how one interacts with the world. There is an innovative software running in the brain, and some versions are faster and more complicated, thereby producing different outcomes. However, we all have license to be inventive. There is no privilege or application to fill out. On planet Earth, humans are the only species that are creating things, like buildings, books, freeways, artworks, etc. You just don't see ants or gorillas creating elaborate cathedrals, or cows coding the internet. So there must, then be a human brain connection with creativity?

An important concept to keep in mind is that the brain is subdivided into two hemispheres, the left and right sides. Each of these structures function for certain tasks, such as, language of the left side of the brain. It has long been thought that the right brain is the creative, poetic and fun side and the left brain is analytical, serious and logical. With more study in neurosciences, there is a reality emerging that creativity involves interaction of many different brain networks. Furthermore, there is science data backing up that most creative people are actually using both sides of the brain together. The most cross talk possible between all parts of the brain and using multiple networks, the more creative one can function.

The neuroscience community has been studying the brain and how it functions on so many paradigms, including what happens if part of the brain is damaged and if a person can continue to do certain activities. There is another method called functional mapping, which measures the brain's activity. There are two functional mapping technologies. The first one is named functional magnetic resonance imaging (fMRI), using magnetic fields to observe blood movement to and from the brain, and of blood bringing fuel materials to parts of the brain that have been active. The second form is called electroencephalography (EEG) and measures the brain's electrical activity.

In a study looking at both EEG and fMRI, brain images were taken from participants while working on tasks for creative thinking. The study demonstrated that when the people came up with creative ideas, "Study participants had synchronized (firing together) brain activity in the frontal cortex and the parietal lobes. In the fMRI study, more creative responses were related to increased activation (or usage) of the frontal cortex in the left hemisphere" (Cavdarkbasha). These results are one of many studies that have concluded there are a many parts of the brain that light up simultaneously with creative thinking.

In looking at the brain's parts, there is no one creative center (see fig. 3). The contributors of the *Frontiers for Young Minds* website show the various parts that can be in action when creativity happens, such as, the frontal cortex, hippocampus, basal ganglia, white matter, and others can make a contribution in the creative process. Neuroscientists in their quest connecting "creative thought processes and the parts of the brain that may process them, have defined creativity as requiring the mixing and remixing of mental representations to create novel ideas and ways of thinking" (Cavdarkbasha).

Along those lines, some argue that you can only be intelligent or creative. But that is not necessarily true. There is a strong correlation between intelligence and creativity. After all, when being creative you are using more of your brain. Intelligence can be defined as the ability to obtain and apply the knowledge. While intelligence and creativity are somewhat similar, a person can be both smart and artsy. There may be something in that intelligence that has a motivation for things novel. In an article entitled, *"Connecting the Dots: Your Brain and Creativity,"* authors, Dita Cavdarkbasha and Jake Kurczek write, "Some Important factors that make people highly creative probably have something to do with personality—things such as openness to new experiences" (Cavdarkbasha, para.16).

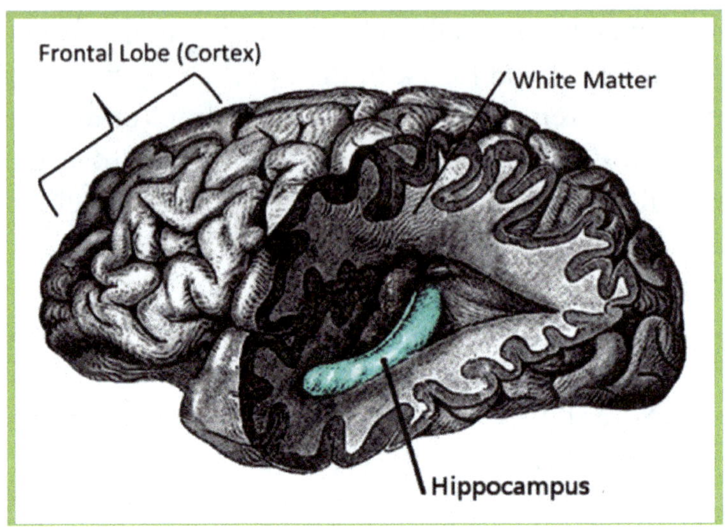


Fig. 3. Different parts of the brain are involved in creativity. Important areas for creative thinking include the following sections of the brain, frontal cortex, basal ganglia, and hippocampus. D. Cavdarbasha, and J. Kurczek. "Connecting the Dots: Your Brain and Creativity." *Frontiers for Young Minds*, kids.frontiersin.org/articles/10.3389/frym.2017.00019. Accessed 25 Mar. 2022.

So what if you think outside of the box and want to create abstract art? Are you crazy?Some people have tried to link mental illness and the creative process together. Scientists have even studied the connection. The link has been called the "mad genius hypothesis" or the "crazy creative hypothesis." In fact, there has been very famous artists in history that suffered from mental illness:

> Vincent Van Gogh (1853–1890, Dutch painter of *The Starry Night*), poet Sylvia Plath (1932–1963, American Pulitzer Prize winning poet, author of *The Collected Poems, The Bell Jar*, and *Ariel*), writer Leo Tolstoy (1828–1910, Russian author, regarded as one of

the greatest authors of all-time, known for *War and Peace* and *Anna Karenina*). (Cavdarkbasha, para. 12)

On the other hand, these are only a few of the countless creative people in the world and only represent a small fraction. Albeit, scientific studies for bipolar disorder, schizophrenia, depression, schizophrenia, addiction, and other illness have been considered in clinic trials. The findings show that super creatives are not necessarily mentally ill, but may think in ways similar to a person suffering from mental illness. According to Nancy Andreasen, a neuroscience of creativity scholar, states, "Many highly creative individuals who were diagnosed with mental illness were not creative because of the mental illness but were creative despite the mental illness working against them" (Andreasen).

So we are crazy or not crazy, but still can be creative? Are we sane and innovative as we make technological products or amazing architecture? We view and interact with the inspiration, process, and creative outcome differently, which makes defining creativity in a universal way very challenging. Steve Jobs reminded us, as cited in Cavdarkbasha, "Even creative people have a hard time seeing the things they think and create as creative" (qtd. in Cavdarkbasha, para. 4).

What also complicates the definition is understanding that creativity comes from various forms such as perforating arts, like music and dance to the visual arts like painting, design, drawing, film making and photography. But does creativity have to just be in the arts? What about the engineer that developed the Keurig coffee maker? Wasn't that design creative as we do not have to mess with messy coffee grounds anymore? What about the individual that created the fibre cement boards? Aren't they creative for coming up with something novel that changes the status quo?

Nevertheless, it does not matter how many approaches to creativity there are, or if we need to define it to a specific field, rather how creativity helps us to understand our lives and various benefits, expressions, and processes is what is paramount. In other words, how does creativity make your life better?

Is there a satisfaction feeling that happens when you create something out of nothing? Is there a connectedness feeling that you have as you reproduce a gorgeous scene in a painting? What about the feeling of happiness and gratefulness that arise as you see your inspiration take form and you breathed it a new life? How do you feel when you share your creation with others and take in their perceptions of it? Creativity has so many components to it and it all starts with a creative moment. Perhaps "a great artist is but a conduit for an expression that resonates with something that is greater than him or herself" (Silva). Which begs the question, does creativity start with the artist or did the inspiration get whispered by another source, like a Muse?

There are many that discuss the creative process with humility and gratefulness. I happen to agree and often say creating art is a privilege that I am so grateful for in my life. Some explain that they had something to do with it, but the creation flowed through them, like an entity on to its own. This is the case with many authors when they just had to write a book and then it just poured out into page after page and they had no idea what was happening. Certainly, this is not the case all the time. However, sometimes it is this exact scenario where there seems to be a separate unseen force, perhaps an unknown genius, that seems to be part of the creation.

There is a sense that there is something larger than the artist working with along side them. It comes through the innovator, however the creation is not exactly from artist or author in its whole. So when the artist crafts beauty, and the poet utters words of romance, what are they doing? Are they creating something from nothing or are they transcribing its essence? Are they recording it in another form, so to speak?

When we are paying attention to the notion of inspiration we are showing tribute to it and breathing in the inspiration and exhaling something, thereby giving it form. This could be the case of transliterating what we are viewing, experiencing, thinking or conjuring. We are recording what is in our mind. Artists may be able to see in a different light, using a different operating lens. Creative thinkers might see things through an individual lens and that's be able to identify things asymmetrically. They are able to read the data with non-conformably ideals in mind, and then interpret it into some formulation. Therefore, with this special lens of perhaps combining objects or techniques that do not necessarily go together is just one of the many ways that a creative type might produce something unique or novel.

So how did the artist come up with the inspiration? Was it formed in one of the physical areas of the brain? Is it a psychological component that the artist had a thought? Or are there other explanations? Which brings up the topic of the muses. Do muses exist and what are their functions in creativity? Do they whisper sweet inspirations into the receptive ear of an artist?

Muses have a long history in relationship to art and music. A muse has three alternative titles: Moisa or Mousa (Greek), and Musa (Latin). Muses can be traced back to the Greco-Roman mythology and religion. They can be described as "any of a group of sister goddesses of obscure but ancient origin, the chief centre of whose cult was Mount Helicon in Boeotia, Greece. They were born in Pieria, at the foot of Mount Olympus" (Britannica). The contributors of *Encyclopedia Britannica* in the "Muse Greek Mythology" section explain, "Very little is known of their cult, but they had a festival every four years at Thespiae, near Helicon, and a contest (*Museia*), presumably—or at least at first—in singing and playing" (Britannica, para. 1). It is theorized that they most likely were:

> The patron goddesses of poets (who in early times were also musicians, providing their own accompaniments), although later their range was extended to include all liberal arts and sciences—hence, their connection with such institutions as the Museum (*Mouseion,* seat of the Muses) at Alexandria, Egypt. (Britannica, para. 1)

Muses are historical creatures even appearing in early works, such as, Homer's *Odyssey,* where Homer summon one or several Muses collectively from time to time. At some point, Muses were considered "one of those vague collections of deities, undifferentiated within the group, which are characteristic of certain, probably early, strata of Greek religion" (Britannica). In Greek mythology, there are nine Muses who are the goddesses of the arts, such as, dance, music, and poetry. They are considered blessed, beautiful and very talented with much allure and grace. They each possess a different artistic gift (see fig. 4).

The nine Greek muses were the daughters of Zeus who is the king of gods, and Mnemosyne who is the goddess of memory. The couple laid together nine nights in a row and each Muse was born each of those nights. In historical legend, the Muses lived on Mount Olympus, Mount Helicon (in Boeotia), or Mount Parnassus. They delighted the gods and humans with their poems, songs and dances. They inspired human artists to superior artistic accomplishments. However, they were not to be questioned, N.S. Gill elaborates, “While they were beautiful to behold and wonderfully gifted, their talents were not to be challenged. Myths regarding challenges to the Muses inevitably end in the challenger losing the challenge and suffering a terrible punishment” (Gill).

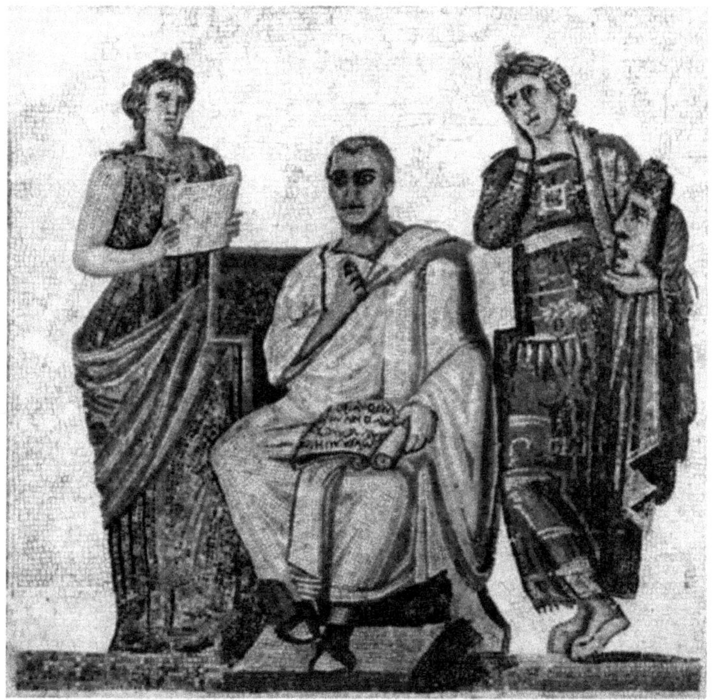

Fig. 4. Virgil with the epic Muse (left) and the tragic Muse (right). Roman mosaic, 2nd–3rd century AD. Currently on exhibition at the Musée Le Bardo, Tunis. *Encyclopedia Britannica*, www.britannica.com/topic/Muse-Greek-mythology. Accessed 25 Mar. 2022.

Muses may or may not be real. I personally have benefited from them. I am so thankful for the inspirations and opportunities I received, so I dare not write they are not real. However, the thing about muses if they are not genuine for the sake of argument, is that they may be the best placebo effect out there.

Once you have been touched by a muse, you know it, and the work is not really something that you could have come up with on your own. No way, there seems to be an outside force propelling the project forward. Steven Pressfield, author of *The War of Art: Winning the Inner Creative Battle*, was quoted in the *Goodreads* website in a section for "Muse Quotes:"

> This is the other secret that real artists know and wannabe writers don't. When we sit down each day and do our work, power concentrates around us. The Muse takes note of our dedication. She approves. We have earned favor in her sight. When we sit down and work, we become like a magnetized rod that attracts iron filings. Ideas come. Insights accrete. (qtd. in Goodreads, para. 5)

There may be some creative producers out there that don't believe in muses, but most of the artists I know, love and respect their creative flow, which may come with the label of "muse." In history, there are countless discussions about the feeling that there is another helping hand at work. Here are some of my favorite *Goodreads* quotations from famous artists discussing these magical benevolent creatures. Prolific author, Stephen King states, "The muses are ghosts, and sometimes they come uninvited" (qtd. in Goodreads, para. 4). Roman Payne explains, "The 'Muse' is not an artistic mystery, but a mathematical equation. The gift are those ideas you think of as you drift to sleep. The giver is that one you think of when you first awake" (qtd. in Goodreads, para. 6). Rob Brezsny writes, "All of us need to be in touch with a mysterious, tantalizing source of inspiration that teases our sense of wonder and goads us on to life's next adventure" (qtd. in Goodreads, para. 20). Lastly, from one of my all time favorite authors from when I was a child, Ray Bradbury states, "To feed your Muse, then, you should always have been hungry about life since you were a child. If not, it is a little late to start" (qtd. in Goodreads, para. 23).

And with that last quote it brings it full circle. In order to create art, you might need to think outside of the box. Perhaps being a little playful, courageous, curious and yes, a tiny bit of craziness is needed when innovating. Plato summarizes this thought very succinctly. He states:

> There is also a third kind of madness, which is possession by the Muses, enters into a delicate and virgin soul, and there inspiring frenzy, awakens lyric....But he, who, not being inspired and having no touch of madness in his soul, comes to the door and thinks he will get into the temple by the help of art--he, I say, and his poetry are not admitted; the sane man is nowhere at all when he enters into rivalry with the madman. (qtd. in Goodreads, para. 24)

# CHAPTER 3: CREATIVE NAME EVOLUTION

As this is partially an autobiographical memoir, it makes sense to start with me as the first creation. Albeit, this is my parent's work, however, as with any artwork piece, it deserves a name. Wistfully, if I can use one word to describe my identity, it would be confusion. You're probably confused why I'm confused about the confusion upon who I am. Yes, I know it's confusing. But what happened early in my life probably led me to the journey of defining and continuing to refine my identity. One might say it had an evolution of its own. I often pondered if with each name change did I create a new persona? Did it help me not think so linear? Did it stretch me into being an ebb and flow of a "person" that could be edited, such as a manuscript or a painting?

It all started when I was born in Argentina. I remember having a large family, a loving mom and dad, a little sister,

Roxana, whom I adored, and wonderful grandparents. I actually had two sets of grandparents, my mom's side, as I remembered were loving, nice and cuddly. I visiting their home and I felt really good there. On my dad's side, the grandparents were a little bit more scary at times as I recall.

In Argentina, I remember having numerous amazing birthday parties to attend, family barbecues, and eating homemade raviolis. As we were Italian, there seemed to be lots and lots of family get togethers. I recall playing with my many cousins and there was a sheer amount of activities revolving the extended family. I recollect loving school and even the uniform I had to wear which looked like an official white lab coat. Everybody look the same, but yet everybody was unique.

I was especially good at writing cursive. Which interestingly in Argentina, kids are taught to write in cursive before they print. This was a source of the beginning of a misalignment, when I was brought to America when I was six years old. It was then, that I had to take first grade over again because I did not know the English language. Additionally, it was a problem that I wrote everything in cursive. The teachers had me write in print, which was very difficult for me. I am sure in today's education there would be some sort of adaptation of my knowledge, but back then all kids had to print, even though cursive was a more complicated way to write, which gets taught in America usually in the third grade.

Our family's immigration to America happened during the 1970s when Argentina was experiencing a violent revolution. As a child, I remembered looking at what seemed to be millions of missing people posters. I did not understand why this was happening, as I was still a young girl. However, I do recall feeling scared that I could go missing as well. You have to understand there were so many posters!

I recently saw those posters again, as in one of my masters program film classes we studying an Argentine film that showed these exact images that have been imprinted in my mind. As an adult, I now understood why I felt such fear. This was a real revolution. There was real violence, and people were being kidnapped and "missing." Which, now days, I realized missing meant killed. Daughters, sons, wives and husbands were slaughtered probably, but nobody knew because they just quietly and silently went missing. So, I think it was probably that had my dad think about following my mom's brother out to the United States. Among the revolution and economic instability, I now understood my father's motivation to get out of the third world country and relocate the family to obtain the American dream. Thereby, having what everyone else wants in the world, a piece of the apple pie.

Furthermore, in my one of film classes for Third Film Cinema which includes movies from third world countries, there was second film that showed many of the images that I carried in my head. I remember watching an intense clip of the revolution that took place in Argentina. What was fascinating to me, and a bit surreal, was the realization was the exact revolution that inspired my parents to immigrate to the United States of America. As small wars like these are not covered in school, I was finally being educated visually and intellectually about circumstances that propelled my life onto another trajectory.

As I watched this film, I realized that someone's creativity helped find a lost piece of the puzzle of my own life. Raw scenes captured on this film create a story of unjust power, and for me a better understanding of my parent's plight. *YouTube* uploader, Kevin Ryan, states:

> Radical and transforming the revolutionary act can reveal as much as subvert hidden truths and hidden powers that oppressed people possess which their oppressors seek to control. In their manifesto for a third cinema, Towards A Third Cinema (1969). The Argentine film makers Fernando Solanas and Octavio Getino proposed that art, and cinema in particular can be a powerful weapon in revealing these truths and aid a revolutionary movement. They point to the connection that art can make with the revolutionary and how, by aiding the revolutionary act it too can become revolutionary. (Ryan)

So, as my early years in Argentina continued, I remember not understanding what was going to happen and I remember missing my father. He came to America for six months on his own trying to figure out what to do and if he was going to bring his family. During those times, I remember spending more time with my mom. I might have even slept in her bed with her and I do remember feeling very close to her as we bonded. I also have memories of spending much time with her parents probably because she felt like she missed my dad, and naturally, she wanted to be more with her family.

One morning, I remember sitting on my Nono's lap looking at his finger that was half missing because he was a masonry work, and at some point he had an accident with a saw. I don't really know what exactly happened, but I just know that I love touching it. He always let me hold it and I just loved holding his hand. But this was an important day because this was the day that my sister, my mom and I were to travel to the USA.

On this morning, I remember him telling me that I was going to go to America on a big airplane. He mentioned, I was a good girl and I needed to continue to be a good sister, and be brave because I was going to be with my dad, mom and sister. He explained I was going to have a new life, and it will be all good. I told him that I did not want to leave and that I liked being here. He said he understood, but that I needed to be with my mother and father. I did not know that was the last time that he and I would talk. I never saw him again after that. It brings me sadness that I did not get to experience this man's love my entire life. Or at least until around when I was sixteen years old when he passed.

When I came to the USA, and attended school, I was very different than most kids born in the United States. For one, I did not know the language. I used cursive instead of printing as that's how they start writing kids in Argentina. Luckily, I had an active mind so I adapted very quickly. I was also placed in an English as a second language class which at some point had a treasure box, as I recall. Oh my gosh, I loved that treasure box. As we studied English, I quickly learned the language and engaged in the activities. I was very motivated as I loved digging for a treasure in the prize chest.

As I study academics, I sometimes chuckle at people saying external prizes don't work, well you know what for this Argentinian girl the external prizes did work. I remember having such wonderful gifts, as these crayons that had different colors that were probably melted together. And I just loved coloring with it seeing a rainbow of colors easily emerge. I also won a monkey puzzle that I must've made one hundred times or more. Those little treasures were comforting to me as I grew up. I think external prizes do work sometimes, maybe not automatically, but yes they do and they did for me. In reflecting about the migration to the US, I often wonder if the way I had to shift everything in my life made me more adaptive and more creative? Or because I was already creative, was I able to integrate faster?

Luckily, I quickly learned the English language. I was probably somewhat fluent in about one and half years, but there was an issue: my name was odd and confusing. See, I was born Claudia Patricia Marcela, so my mom would call me Claudia. My dad would call me Patri, which is short for Patricia and in English, it translates into Patty. And so the confusion started.

I once asked my mom why she called me Claudia, but then my dad would call me something different. She told me that it was because they couldn't decide what to name me, therefore they named me both. My mother explained that she named me after an Argentinian magazine that was something like *Vogue*. Who knows where Marcela came from, but in any event they named me all three names. Even more confusing, when they addressed me, each would use the name that they individually picked. Oh my gosh, do you know how confusing this is for someone?

In any event at school, I was Claudia. At the time, I did not know what bullying was. Having learned more about it as I raised my children and worked as a teacher, I was trained in how to deal with bullying behavior. Recalling how I felt growing up, I believe that my name was a source of me being ridiculed. The kids at school would call me dirt Claude. And I remember feeling confused why they now were calling me yet “another” name. I was this little girl that probably was very different, dressed in a pretty dress, but being called dirt clod. Yes, my feelings were hurt.

So a couple of years later, I said that it’s OK. I don't have to be a dirt clod, I have a different name. My name is also Patri, translated into Patty, so then Patty was born in the academic world. I wonder if this is when I started to see things outside of the box? Why does it have to be a certain way, when we can just do something differently?

Problem solved right? No, then the first name initial issue came up. Here's the problem, at that time, the academic school computer or paperwork did not allow for a middle name to be used as a first name. So what's the girl's first name, Claudia, but she doesn't want to be called Claudia, my mom would try to explain as I translated her words to the school secretary. And, so somewhere in a school office, my name started to come with an initial as my first name.

Now C. Patricia became an entity. Are you counting? I think, I now have three identities, four if you count Patri and Patty as separate. Wow, there are so many variations in just a name. Again in contemplation, this might have been the start of me thinking that things are not as they appear. There are many forms for the same item, all of which are neither right or wrong, just different variations, just like Claude Monet's waterlilies paintings.

I was realizing that through my different name changes, I was also refining and defining who I was. Interestingly, as I grew as a person and artist, my name would take another shift as it did early in my childhood. Although I felt confused, I did learn a lesson in creativity, which is basically, you get to edit and recreate as you see fit.

There's a story that one of my painting teachers like to tell and that is the life of the painting. Basically, the painting has different stages in its development, and one of those phases is the ugly duckling stage. Painters are all too familiar with this point, where you know how it is going to turn out, but it is just not there yet. In a way, in parenting, that might be considered the teenage years, where the child is trying to individualize and seek out their own identity. Perhaps, I did that for most of my life. Maybe this was also part of my artistic journey, to morph and recreate and accept, and grow and edit some more.

As I started to have my own children, I took such care in picking out their names all the while consulting various baby name books. I realized at some point, I could do the same with myself. Iman Baobeid, wrote an informative article named "On the Importance of Names" for *The University of British Columbia Equity and Inclusion Office.* She writes:

> Our names are an incredibly important part of our identity. They carry deep personal, cultural, familial, and historical connections. They also give us a sense of who we are, the communities in which we belong, and our place in the world. This is why mispronunciations, misuse of our preferred/common names, or misgendering can negatively affect and possibly hurt and impact a sense of belonging on campus. (Baobeid)

With looking back at the past, I can see how my design creations, such as, gardens, kitchen remodels, construction home additions, and so on, were created under a certain name, and how perhaps a little of that name's personality was in charge at that time. For instance, I remember dropping the "C" with C. Patricia Gray because there was a social security issue, and it seemed that computer systems did not know what to do with a first initial as a first name. Then with the name, Patricia M. Gray, I had the most publications because I wrote freelance writing and photojournalism under that name. This was also the name that I was using when I started Gray Designs in 2012.

Then, in 2015, I had a big decision to make. I was making a very large glass order for a hotel, and at that time my work was being confused with another glass artist using a similar name. What was funny about this situation, is that even my sister was being confused with our separate websites. So it was during one of these birthdays I had (let's just say 29 years, ha ha) that I realized I had all these different identities, however they weren't truly my identity. Furthermore, I was now being confused with someone else's work which was a little frustrating.

I recall working hard on the glass projects and I decided that it was good timing to make a solid shift as I was glass fusing my name and website to every piece. I realized this was the time right time to commit to my own identification. But which name do I pick? Wait I thought, I actually have my own identity. Why don't I go back to my birth name, Claudia?

Some of you may relate to what I experienced. For those of you perhaps struggling to create with just the right artist name. Or whether you are trying to come up with a catchy name for your company, there are many resources to help you. I remember going to the computer and researching artist names and name changes, etc. I also discussed my ideas with my family. I also realized that I would also need a legal name change in my particular situation. I pondered many points, like these listed in the *DYI Musician* website:

Tips On How To Choose Your Artist Name

1. Your name should be original.
2. Don't call yourself the thing that you DO.
3. Your artist name probably shouldn't have parentheses or a colon.
4. Be careful with funky spellings.
5. Limit the number of monikers you use.
6. Know your brand, and match it to your name.
7. Know your brand, and match it to your name. (DYI Musician)

Like the ugly duckling stage of the painting, I was emerging on to the next phase. It was then that I realized that my mom had compromised with my father in calling me a specific name. However, really that is not who I was and it caused much confusion for so many decades. I actualized that I needed to make this correct for both of us. So I went through a formal name change and embracing my birthright, my birth name, and gave my mom the gift of validating her choice over my name. Now, after a court document was recorded, I was legally my birth named Claudia Patricia Marcela Gray. OK, I still kept my old married name but still close. I called my mom in Argentina with this news and she was actually so pleased and delighted.

Additionally, I was happy also because in a way I became born again with a true identity that no one else could be confused by; after all do you know many Claudia Patricia Marcela Grays? I know, I know, there's a famous author named Claudia Gray. Well, at least she is not creating glass art in my region.

Of special note, is that now days, I often use the nickname Claude when I want to be gender neutral, I thought this was also full circle with when I was little girl being called dirt clod. But here as a grown woman, if I am in a very public site, I might go by the name Claude. Which reminds me of a very inspirational artist of mine, Claude Monet, so it's good enough for Claude it's good enough for me!

# CHAPTER 4: CREATIVITY FORMS COMMUNITY

One thing I have noticed is that no matter where you are in the world, art brings people together. It starts at a young age. For the most part, art is a form of play and positive experience for children. Art classes and instruction bring kids together. Additionally, they walk away with something that they created and can be proud of. The creative adventures benefits are not only for the students.

I personally have received much joy, knowledge, and found great friends as I volunteered in the various school art programs. I was thrilled and felt very lucky to participate with my four children in their respective classrooms. Throughout the eight years that I helped out in fabulous programs like Art Masters and Art in Action at a couple of different schools and countless classrooms, I shared happy moments with the students, teachers and fellow volunteers. Additionally, all these efforts and experiences formed a community. We were the art volunteers, ready to get messy with a smile on our faces!

I have noticed throughout my travels, that this forming of a community takes place as well. I have been lucky enough to be on countless backpacking trips, photography workshops, or touring a different country in search of beautiful photography subject matter. It never ceases to amaze me that even though we may be shooting the same scene, there is a camaraderie that is shared, and it seems like we all have a different perspective on the scene or a different angle. We end up not getting the same shot, because technical settings on each individual camera can be different. Many times, we share F stop or white balance settings. I remember one time when I was hiking with two guides in a Costa Rica jungle where we were coming up on a waterfall and I was looking in a different direction. It was then that one of the men showed me what was coming up. Wow - a rainbow made on a sunny day from the waterfall mist (see fig. 5). I may have gotten to that scene, but in photography each nanosecond counts. And I remember thinking even though he doesn't have a camera he wants to share the moment with me which is priceless. Even though I was the photographer on that hike, he was helping me create my images. So I took the shot and I showed him, and we were so happy at the same time. This happened a lot when people share a snippet in time with similar emotions.

There is even a neuroscience term for shared emotions in a crowd. Emotional contagion is a social event involving the emotional spontaneous spread and related behaviors. This feeling transfer can occur in a large group or from one person to another. These emotions are shared through verbal, non-verbal, implicitly or explicitly. The same phenomenon often

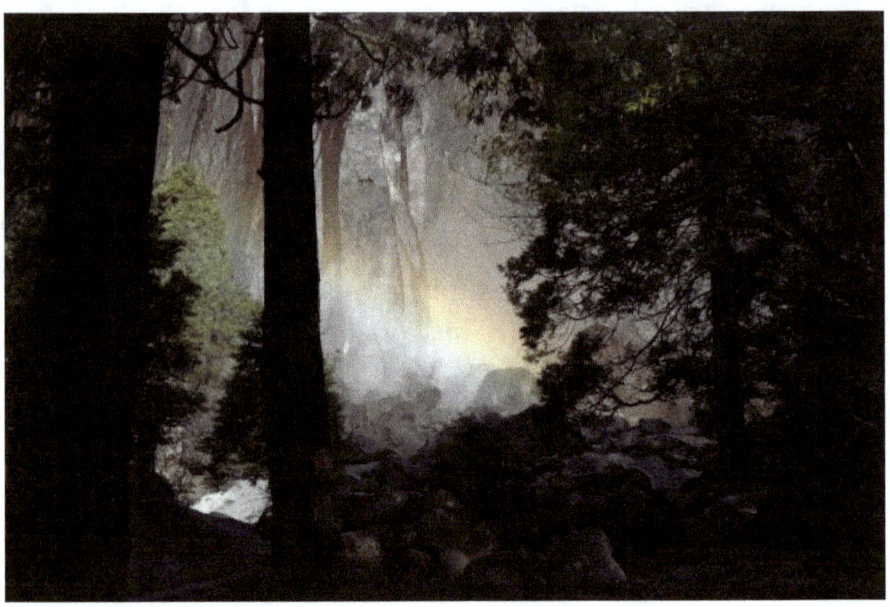

Fig. 5. Costa Rican jungle, low hanging rainbow from the waterfall spray. Claudia Gray. *Costa Rican Mist*. 2013, collection of the artist.

happens at concerts, where the whole crowd is moving up and down with the sound of the music or at a photo shoot awaiting Mother Nature to put on her show (see fig. 6). If you look around most of the people are enjoying the same type of emotions. What I am talking about actually has a name, The Emotional Contagion Hypothesis which was first coined by Elaine Hatfield in 1993. Hatfield defined it as, "The tendency to automatically mimic and synchronize expressions, vocalizations, postures, and movements with those of another person's and, consequently, to converge emotionally" (qtd. in Nickerson, para. 8).

Although this might seem like a novel neuroscience and psychology situation, marketers and advertising companies have been using emotional contagion for its benefit. Charlotte Nickerson writes, "Advertisers and technology companies have long utilized emotional contagion

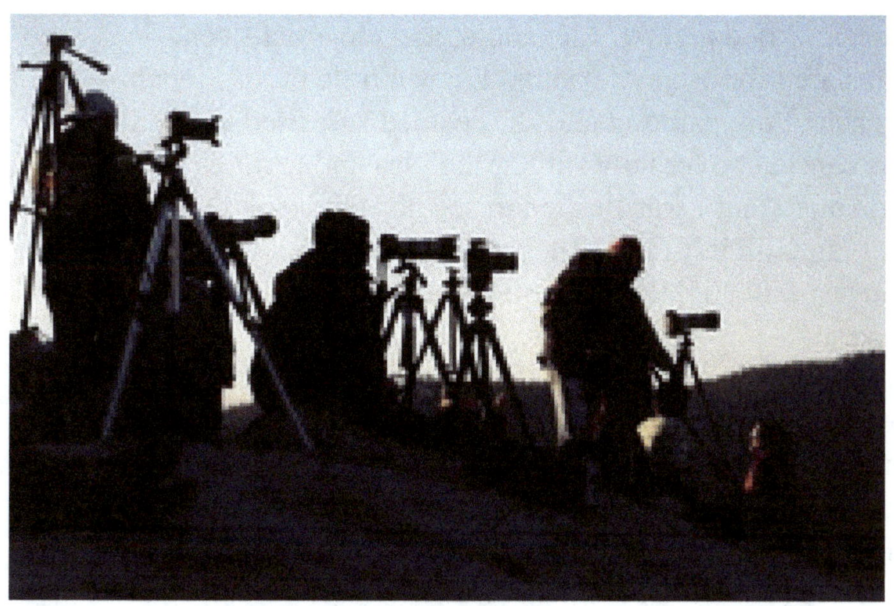

Fig. 6. Yosemite National Park, Glacier Point, waiting for sunset to light up Half Dome. Claudia Gray. *Glacier Point Photo Frenzy*, 2013 collection of the artist.

to associate positive feelings with their brands. This has been derided by some critics as 'emotional engineering'" (Nickerson, para. 1).

I have always loved travel, and one of the things I invested in with my art sales was a travel slush fund, as I would call it. Because I took travel photographs, it made sense to save and reinvest in my company and travel experiences to help with obtaining more shots around the world. It was on one of these trips, funded mostly by my own art, that my daughter and I were traveling in the South of France and we came about a little village with many art galleries. We went into one gallery that had many tree paintings. These paintings seemed familiar to me and I pulled out my phone and showed my daughter my early painting from 2012. The artist and I started to speak, but we couldn't understand ourselves as I spoke English and she spoke

French. My daughter, Alexandra, and the artist's son translated for us as Alexandra knew a little bit of French. We looked at my painting and she seemed surprised and said that she can't get over how similar the idea and textures were. I explained that I was thrilled to see how she took that one idea and ran with it, as her gallery was full with very large canvases all slightly different but almost all with this same theme.

We shared a very special moment in human and artistic connection as the four of us in two separate languages discussed creativity. Emotion contagion was at work again throughout the different countries. "The recognition of emotions according to facial expressions is universal in world cultures (Brown, 2004), and facial expressions can communicate emotions ranging from approval to expectations and emotions" (Nickerson, para. 4).

The four of us discussed ideals, such as, does one creative inspiration reach one artist or various artist at the same time throughout the world? I explained that in my view, I believe that there's an inspiration that a muse might throw out to various artists throughout the planet to make sure that that the paradigm gets put into form. The problem is that not every artist listens. For instance, how many times have we had an inspiration and it just escapes? However, that item, in my belief, needs to be created still whether by you or someone else. Thereby, I am a firm believer that the Muses have different people create at the same time. Albeit, there's always somebody that does a better job, and runs with it, so to speak.

In this case, I gave many kudos to the artist who took the tree inspiration with the texture technique and made it her own. Interestingly, she used paint chips and I had use joint compound. She then continued to explore the idea and created a whole gallery of those types of paintings. In the end, the Muses picked several people, I was one of them, but I only created one painting, whereas, this artist created so many. So if this was a tennis match she wins. But we all won that afternoon, as we had a very long discussion and a beautiful creative moment which ended up with big international hugs and shared emotion contagion.

This has happened to me at several situations around the world. Another time, when I was in Spain, there was an artist who happened to be born in Argentina, just like me. Her life took her to Japan and she learned art there. She came back with a variety of different methods and started a studio in Spain. We instantly became fast friends as we discussed Argentina, Japan and what it's like to create in Spain. I talked to her about my creations and what I was making with glass. Because Spanish is my first language, I was able to have a very fluid conversation with her. We felt united and again that afternoon ended with a big hug and smiles. What surprised me is that no matter where I am in the world, art actually does unite people. Artists, generally, are usually very open and receptive people and there is some sort of collaboration that happens naturally.

I remember another trip where a similar emotional creativity took place in Berlin. This time, it was my daughter, Olivia, and I were on a self made bike tour of the city. Because she wanted to see the historical parts of the area, and I wanted to take photos of them, we decided to rent bicycles and create our own “Mum and Liv” trek. In this situation, not being a fan of a tour company’s exacting scheduling, after all sometimes, the photo opportunity does not line up with their itinerary, we felt free and spontaneous. It's these moments that sometimes create precious moments that could not have been experienced unless present at the right time and the right place.

Together we created a loosely timed tour that was about fifty miles on bicycle. We were both active, enthusiastic and ready for the challenge. One of the things that I try to keep in mind with this in particular bicycle trip was that I was supposed to be submitting work for a "Divergent Travel" themed juried photography show at a local gallery. Therefore, while enjoying the sightseeing, exercise and my daughter's company, I was also on the hunt for items that were dissonant in nature for my show's entry submission. I must admit, Berlin did not disappoint, as I was able to get two of my travel photos accepted into the juried show exhibition.

A must on our tour was the Berlin Wall. At this location, I was surprised to see how much tourism had taken a hold of the Checkpoint Charlie area which was the crossing point between West Berlin and East Berlin during the cold war. I wanted something more special and intimate for my photojournalism. So, we continued to several stops on the Berlin Wall, after all, it is nearly twenty-seven miles long. After hundreds of shots, and empathically trying to understand the gist of what I was seeing and perhaps what the previous people during the oppression years were feeling, I selected one of the shots that captured the essence of the emotions. I named the photograph, "A Glimpse Of Freedom" (Gray).

This shot was special to me because I made careful decisions on the cloud being shown through the little broken piece of the wall. Technically, this was a bit challenging, as Berlin is a busy city, with many bystanders, cars, and visual noise all around the wall. The sky and clouds and where I stood had to be just right. Intuitively I knew this was a special part of the wall, and I felt connected to it. I took many shots in various forms of this location from different angles with the fast moving clouds. The shot that I finally selected is the one I ended up submitting. It ended up being accepted by the Divergent Travel juried show and was also featured at another gallery (see fig. 7).

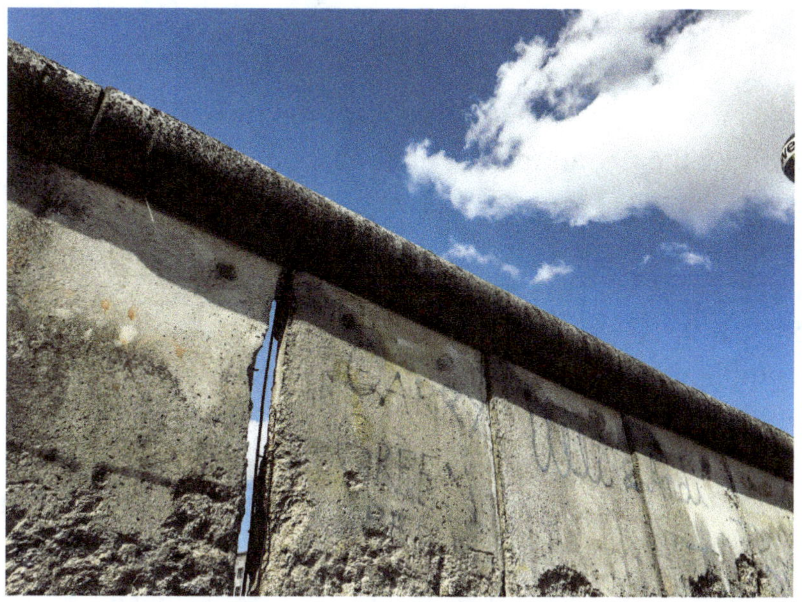

Fig. 7. Claudia Gray. *Glimpse of Freedom*. 2019, collection of the artist.

At the time, I really didn't give much thought about why I was needing to convey emotions through this photograph or how my brain was functioning. I did know that I wanted to choose a very heavy and daunting frame for it so it could further have the feeling of oppression. As I learned more about mirror neurons and continued my fascination with neuroscience, I understood a little bit more. Joshua Sarinana wrote in article entitled, *Photography and the Feelings of Others: From Mirroring Emotions to the Theory of Mind,* "Photography is powerful because we can place ourselves into the perspective of those we see in an image. Whether it's street photography, photojournalism or portraiture, we use photography to understand ourselves in relation to people around us" (Sarinana, para. 1). Furthermore, "Our ability to identify with and imagine someone else's point of view is deeply ingrained into the architecture of our brain. Photography plays a unique role in triggering the network of brain regions that underlie empathy" (Sarinana, para. 3).

What Sarinana was talking about became further validated a couple of years after I took this shot as one of my visitors saw the photograph at my home and expressed being instantly connected to it. He explained to me that his grandfather was actually behind the Berlin wall. He said he could feel what his grandfather was feeling perhaps being trapped behind it as he looked at my image. That photographed catapulted him back to his grandfather's potential experiences and emotions. He also commented favorably on the heavy frame with the lines that symbolized a jail like situation. My guest was feeling what I had originally wanted to convey in the photograph. I had chills running up and down my legs.

Perhaps other people at the gallery exhibitions felt the same pangs, I do not know, but having at least one person tell me their story and how they connected with it, was priceless for me as a human, artist, and photographer, I felt that my self imposed assignment was completed. I realized at that moment, that it's just icing on the cake to be exhibited in galleries. When you are able to share your work, it can reach a larger audience and be viewed by many. Moreover, when your creations touch another human being, well, that feeling is hard to describe. It is truly awe-inspiring and very satisfying. Isn't this why we create art, to express and share our feelings and evoke emotions in the viewers?

It is not only after the image is taken that there is a common emotion shared. This can also happen when the photograph is being shot or an artwork is being worked on. One of the best examples I can share is on this same Mum Liv Bike Tour of Berlin. We had finished with the Berlin Wall and we were on our way through a beautiful park on our way to the Berlin capital buildings. All of a sudden as we were riding around the beautiful architectural buildings we heard a lot of sirens. When I say a lot, I mean like nothing I have heard before. My Wilderness First Responder training kicked in and I quickly started to survey the scene. Were we in danger? What is happening? My first thought was oh my gosh there's a bomb! Luckily, that was not the case, and what was happening was a demonstration. Then I was asking myself is this a peaceful demonstration or are there going to be things thrown? What do we do?

We felt comfortable enough to stay and view the demonstration. There were lots of young peoples and many parents. They were saying something in German and I was not sure what was happening. Then my photojournalism instincts kicked in and once I knew my daughter and I were safe, I got off of my bike and started taking pictures. I asked her if she was OK if I moved around a little bit and she said sure go ahead.

I started to get that special feeling I get when something is telling me this is important to take note. Could it be one of my Muses? Perhaps, they are quite amazing. “Be in the moment,” I heard in my mind. Then my photographic technical experience started to take hold of me. This is sometimes where I lose time and my breathing starts being more slowly succinct because I do not want my images to be blurry. I looked at my daughter from time to time making sure she was ok, and then I started to move around to secure good angles. I was looking up and around, scanning the scene, making sure I had the protestor's signs and capturing their facial expressions. The shots were good but not good enough. I was not satisfied. It could be better my Muses whispered.

Finally, as I was moving around there was more and more photographers arriving at the scene. I quickly realized that I was one of the first photographers at the location because my daughter and I just happen to be at the right place, at the right time. Now, more and more photojournalist including news people with their big TV vans started to show up.

Because I was one of the first few, I was already in the front and I was able to move around. As I was taking my images, there was another European photographer along side me. Instead of being competitive, we looked at each other, smiled and nodded to each other. Somehow, I had developed this nod, which has been eternally useful as I take photographs in foreign places or even at home at Buddhist events with most of the participants speaking another language like Tibetan, Vietnamese and Chinese. This universal nod I frequently employ is a sign for "Isn't this awesome! Let's enjoy the shots and this moment together!" Because it is a non-threatening nod and I have a smile, more often than not, it is returned right back to me.

So going back to this European photographer that most likely spoke German and I spoke English (and Spanish), we had a mutual undiscussed understanding, "Let's take fantastic photographs and share the moment." I don't know if he felt the same way I did, as it seemed like we were a team even though we were complete strangers. But we were peacefully parallel playing like two happy toddlers in a sandbox. We were taking shots, moving our cameras from left to right, up and down. We shifted and danced around each other as we both tried to get the right angle for the waving flag and the protestors moving signs.

At one point, I walked away from my newfound comrade in search for a better angle. And then there it was: the building, at a diagonal, with beautiful German students pronouncing their protests, with a sign visible, in English to boot, and the flag perfectly visibly waving in the background. Oh my Gosh! I had the amazing shot I was after (see fig. 8).

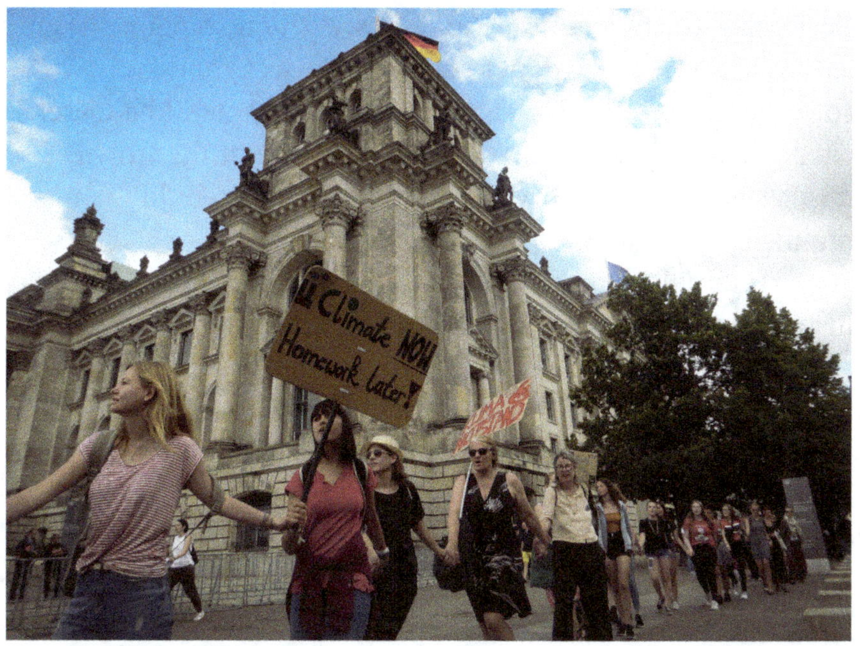


Fig. 8. Claudia Gray. *Klimaschutz, Deutsche Studenten Protestieren*. 2019, collection of the artist.

I was happy and there was a thrill going through me. It was then that I looked behind me as there was commotion. Was I in danger now? No, it was merely a news crew setting up shop right at my angle exactly where I was standing. Well, the nod served me well again, and as I was now part of this community of photojournalist and TV reporters, I felt connected to the German crews, people and the protestors. Somehow, intuitively, I knew that this was a special moment that this crowd, bystanders and photographers were sharing.

I wanted to also show my genuine feelings of belonging together and peacefulness. Sarinana elaborates on this social norm, "Imitation is automatic and a basic requirement for developing practical social skills, like empathy. When we see the expression of other peoples faces there is an unconscious activation of the same muscles" (Sarinana). As an example, he writes, "When someone is sad and frowns you too will active frown muscles and feel similarly to the person you're looking at, granted to a lesser extent. If you were to prevent the activation of the frown muscles then your ability to perceive sadness would diminish" (Sarinana).

Internally, I felt great feelings of grateful for being at this location. Art does create community. Certainly, there were many things at play at this scene. Most importantly, the message that the student protestors were trying to convey which was climate change must happen. I wanted to help them and spread their message. I also felt thankful that I paid attention to all those photography workshops. It was in one of those classes where a teacher told me that my best tool in my photo bag are my feet. Get up and move, and use those feet, I heard my Muses shout! And, because I listened, I had probably the best angle at the location, good enough for a German news van to pull up right behind me. I was satisfied that I picked that location first and on my own. Nonetheless, it didn't matter. We all can share the same location and take our shots. I was understanding that we all go back and report what we experienced to our different communities. I felt grateful that I was among these European photographers and I was accepted. A smile and a nod can go a long way to collaboration and acceptance.

By the way, that shot was also accepted into the Divergent Travel juried show and it was also exhibited at a second gallery. Those students made the German news shows, that night and their message continued to be broadcasted each time my photograph was being exhibited. This is another example of how art binds people together and messages are spread worldwide.

It is widely accepted that groups have a tendency to make people feel like they belong. Before I became a professional artist, there was a special artist friend that invited me to their studio. The person was an engineer-type by profession and had exhibited amazing artwork at coveted Laguna Beach art shows, however, no longer sold artwork. Now creating for just fun, the artist learned I had always wanted to do art and I received an invitation to create at the studio with other art lovers once a week.

Somewhere along the line, this community was the beginning of what I needed to start art becoming one of my primary activities in my life. Art has a tendency to make people feel like they belong. Even London's Tate Museum recognizes this and they have a podcast called *The Art of Belonging What does it mean to belong?* Their subtitle says, "Artists, writers and poets explore the human stories behind art and belonging" (Tate). In the Tate's episodes, they state they explore "What it means to belong. How can art make us feel part of something, how can it help us to connect with ourselves and others? Hear artists, an author and a poet reflect on their experiences of art and belonging" (Tate).

I did not need to listen to the Tate's podcast, as perhaps this podcast wasn't in existence back in 2010 or so. However, I will always be grateful for the invitation of me being a part of the fold. There were many lessons learned during this timeframe. I remember many times of unintentionally frustrating the lead artist as perhaps I was not as neat nor educated in how to use the materials and perhaps, even the space. After all, they were a trained formal artist, and I just wanted to play. They were amazingly talented and very precise with drawings and paintings of elaborate landscapes and technical insect artwork. Contrastingly, I had no formal training, but loved the idea of creating, and it just sounded like plain ol' fun to me! As it was, I had a beginner's mind and touch. I was playful and enchanted. And I was literally, giddy about it. Oh my, I thought, I finally get to play at art, without any kids, or schools or rules, or so I thought.

At one point we worked with painting tile. The artist brought me up to speed and I learned about wax reliefs and how to add paint inside of each line with one color. I remember feeling instantly constrained by the lines and having to only choose a single color. My Muses and perhaps a bit of my Punk Rock girl still inside of me were whispering, "Wait - coloring inside the lines, no that's not creative… that's stifling." Nevertheless, in my early pieces I listened to the instructions, silently whimpering inside as I applied one color inside of the wax reliefs.

At some point, I don't recall exactly when I started to follow my instincts and perhaps I might have been a bit creatively daring and did not follow the rules. For instance, I started to mix colors together making gradient color combinations. The artist explained that depending on the glazes it may not work. However, I did not know any better, and I wanted to play and explore. This reminds me of Pablo Picasso's famous quote, "Every child is an artist, the problem is staying an artist when you grow up" (Johnson).

During the creation of these pieces, I especially liked how one color would blend into another. What was interesting about this story is that I realized that different artists have a different continuum of artistic roles, inspiration, methods, abilities and talents. For instance, for me it was fun to see everything meld together, for another, it may need to be a very precise method of application and use of medium in a particular way (see fig. 9).

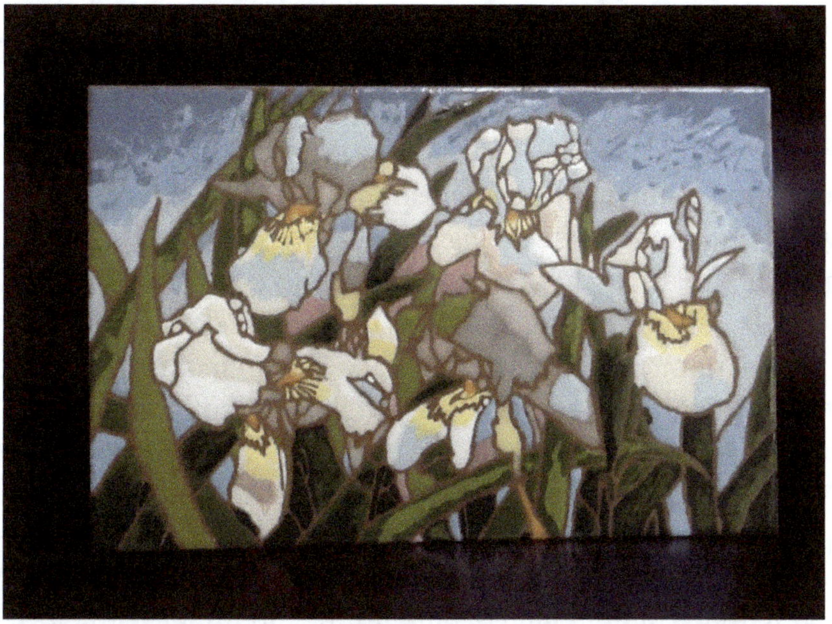

Fig. 9. One of my ceramic tiles I made using my different colors within the wax relief line, Claudia Gray. *Orchid Tile Art*. 2012, collection of the artist.

After sometime had passed, the artist showed me a tile that they created blending colors within the wax reliefs. Although, I did not create this technique, and most likely they used this method previously, they tried it once again. The piece showed a wave by the ocean and it looked lovely! I was surprised, and I will never truly know how our time together influenced the creation of this piece. Perhaps, in a way, I might have inspired them to feel more free and not stay within the lines. They commented that now pleased with the outcome, they may consider using this method in future pieces. Another ideal that this experience taught me was that within an art community, there's room for individuality and learning from each other. I also learned to trust and follow my own inspiration because that is how you create your own style and unique look.

At some point, I had visited a Laguna Beach show that had another tile artist, and surprisingly, this artist took the same flow of colors and combining different colors in one wax relief area like I had done. I did report back to my artist friend and realized that I wasn't crazy after all. Besides, according to the neuroscience studies, you can be creative while being crazy. All joking aside, this example is yet another situation where people create alike and differently with the same medium, and truly there is no right nor wrong.

After doing more reading and research in my masters studies, I learned that many big artists have collaborated and enjoyed spending time together. For instance, Ansel Adams had social connections and creativity continued to grow as he spent time in New Mexico with fellow artists like Georgia O'Keeffe and Paul Strand. Among the artists in his crowd was also Alfred Stieglitz who eventually would give Adams' first exhibitions. Stieglitz had a gallery in New York and helped both O'Keeffe and Adams become famous.

Ansel Adams continued to further his career by collaborating with fellow photographers, such as Dorothea Lange and Walker Evans in their quest for social and political change through art. Adams also aligned himself with the Sierra Club, an environmental organization founded by John Muir. Adams felt that the Sierra Club's mission of protecting wilderness areas, which included his beloved Yosemite, connected with what he felt was right in his heart. Continuing with other projects, he found himself in places other than nature like when Adams photographed internment camp life of Japanese-American people during World War II.

Among the many projects Adams had his hands in was the founding of the Group f/64 which is a photographer association embracing "pure" photography (meaning sharp focus and full tonal range). Not only was Adams one of the founders, but also a master of this style of photography. Marvin J. Rosen and David L. Devries elaborate in their book, *Photography & Digital Imaging*, "A founding member of the f/64 group, Adams was a master of revealing with impeccable clarity and precision the formal beauty of natural objects, from trees, roots, and Driftwood to landscapes of the grandest scale" (26).

In 1940, Ansel Adams with Fred Archer developed the Zone System. This is a way of adjusting the photograph's exposure thereby showcasing the image's shadows and highlights. Their system divides a scene into ten zones on the tonal scale where every tonal range is assigned a zone. Basically, each zone is slightly different from the one before it by one stop, and from the one following it by another one stop. Thereby, every zone change is always the same one stop difference. This has changed how photography is managed by the photographers as this system enables photographers to maximize optimal exposure, furthermore, mapping out the various tonal regions or luminance of objects. It is the first system to manipulate light, and is a crucial part of photography's history and developments. Michael Freeman, author of the book, *Perfect Exposure: The Professional's Guide to Capturing Perfect Digital Photographs*, details how the Zone System works excellent for the hue, value and saturation (HVS) of an image. He writes, "Ansel Adams' 10-

zone division is perceptually spot on, as each of the zones refers to a brightness level that triggers a particularly response in the HVS" (134).

Adams helped bring photography into the exclusive world of fine art. The appreciation of photography as a fine art form was solidified by the 1960s. Adams' photographs were widely exhibited in numerous important museums and galleries throughout the USA. The Metropolitan Museum of Art in New York city hosted a retrospective exhibit in 1974 to honor the successful career of Adams. The demand was continued to be high for his iconic images. Consequently, during the 1970s, Adams spent much of his time in the darkroom printing negatives.

But its not just famous artists that get together and make fabulous new techniques or products. Art and community go hand in hand. I know that there's a certain camaraderie that happens when someone wants to make something or is fascinated and passionate about a certain topic. For instance, I love water lilies and as I often paint them. During that phase, I received many waterlily photographs from another fellow artist. She would send them and say something like thinking about you, maybe you can paint this one too.

One of the things that I realized is that I do that myself with my son, Tommy, who happens to be a very gifted artisan himself. Tommy just loves to work with wood and so whenever I see a really cool wood project or an outstanding wood furniture piece, I snap a photo of it and send it to him. On a recent trip that I shared with my girlfriend, I did just that, I took a picture of some creative wood thing and sent it to my son. I explained to her how he makes all these different hand-carved wood bowls and wood furniture as I showed her a few of his creations. So then she said well I know of a store that has really great wood stuff. So we walked across the mall, and we went inside the store. Sure enough, they did. So we snapped some photographs and sent them to him. I realized that now my friend was now part of the community of helping this young artist succeed. As we sent him our photographs, perhaps he would be inspired to create his own take on what he is viewing.

One of the most obvious things that creates community is a creative handmade gift. How sweet is it when you get something handcrafted? Not only did the person have the inspiration to make it, they dedicated making this work for you, and they put time and effort into it. Schools and art teachers know how special this is. In a way, it's a special snippet in time that this child can make something memorable to keep for many years to come.

Those special keepsakes are the items that just can't make it into the recycling bin or trashcan. Most parents keep those special objects on display or tucked away in a treasure box. According to Caroline Soriano, author of *Why You Should Give Handmade Gifts When You Want To Make Someone Feel Extra Special -- Benefits Of Handmade Presents*, she writes, "Handmade gifts often let the receiver feel that they are loved. They think that the person giving the gift has spent enough time thinking about what they want, something that shows their personality or interest" (Soriano).

And so, we have put a value of "priceless" to a creative object made from an unknown artist, your child. I have done that many of times. I still adore the special handprint plates and clay creations my children have gifted me. That type of creativity has a special meaning and is most definitely priceless. Sure, it may not be a fantastic piece of art nor technically correct, and perhaps it may be really messy looking, but in the eye of the beholder it is a masterpiece. It's that type of art that creates community. “In addition, a handmade gift lets someone feel extra special because rather than giving a store-bought present, you chose to put your time creating something. Without a doubt, the person who will receive it will feel nothing but good vibes” (Soriano).

This reminds me of a time when I was the recipient of a handcrafted gift which will be forever treasured, as I know how much time and effort it took. Soriano agrees, and elaborates on this point of time being part of the gift giving, “A handmade gift is a fail-proof gift you can give on any occasion. It’s a unique way of telling your recipient that they are special. After all, the gift itself took time to be created and nothing spells love better than T-I-M-E” (Soriano).

Tommy, my son, also loves to shape surfboards out of foam core, a skill he learned and taught at his college. One Mother’s Day, I was presented with a handmade surfboard that Tommy made, and had the other three siblings paint. He then glassed it and put fins on it as well as a leash. I couldn't believe that he went through all that time and trouble as I know how many hours it takes to fabricate a surfboard. The four kids had me close my eyes, and when they were ready, I got to open my eyes and see all four of them carrying the surfboard towards me (see fig. 10). Priceless, awe-inspiring and my heart absolutely melted. They know how much I love then sun, and they remembered that as they had painted a sun on it. The colors and everything about it was amazing to me. I was definitely, a happy surfer girl, but I also felt blessed and honored as a mother.

Of special note, was that he also said that this handcrafted gift comes with an outing to go surfing with Tommy. This has been something that we both really enjoy, and somewhere along the line it had been a long time since we were out in the water together. So I was so excited. The adding included his girlfriend, Tommy and me. I told him that I really needed to have some baby waves since it's been a while, so we decided on Cowell Cove in Santa Cruz (see fig. 11). The spot was very special to me as this is where I first learned how to surf. This was a creative gift that was extremely full circle. As we paddled out at some point we decided to take a party wave together, and I got up on the wave and so did he and I thought in my brain oh my gosh I have to really seal this memory in my long-term memory as this is an unbelievable situation. Incredibly, as I was riding the wave and thinking this, I looked over to him and Tommy was riding the wave and doing a handstand! I chuckled and I thought OK now you really have to get this into long-term memory! What a great creative gift from beginning to end.

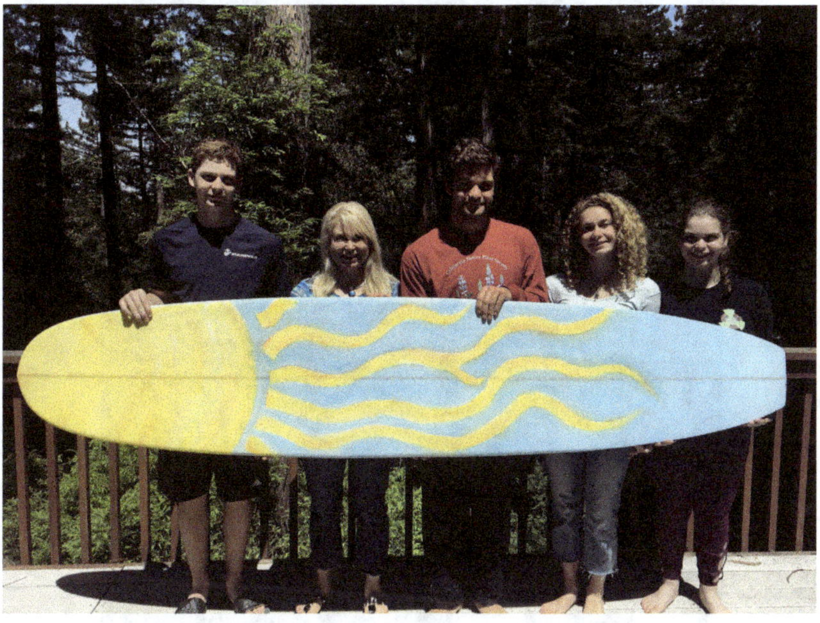

Fig. 10. From Left: Jack, Claudia, Tommy, Olivia and Alexandra, Mother's Day 2019. Claudia Gray. *Mother's Day Surf*, 2019, collection of the artist.

In reflection, Tommy's gift had a ripple effect. For instance, the other kids got to paint something that I will always treasure, his girlfriend got to hang out with us and surf a little bit, but she was also part of this community that was being created by the handcrafted gift. And then of course, the story continues as I perhaps talk about it with friends and it ends up being one of those life stories that you really love to share with people. Overall, it's a story that makes people just feel super good, in surf language that would be sharing the stoke. Or making people feel stoked. And it all stemmed from Tommy's inspiration and putting form to it.

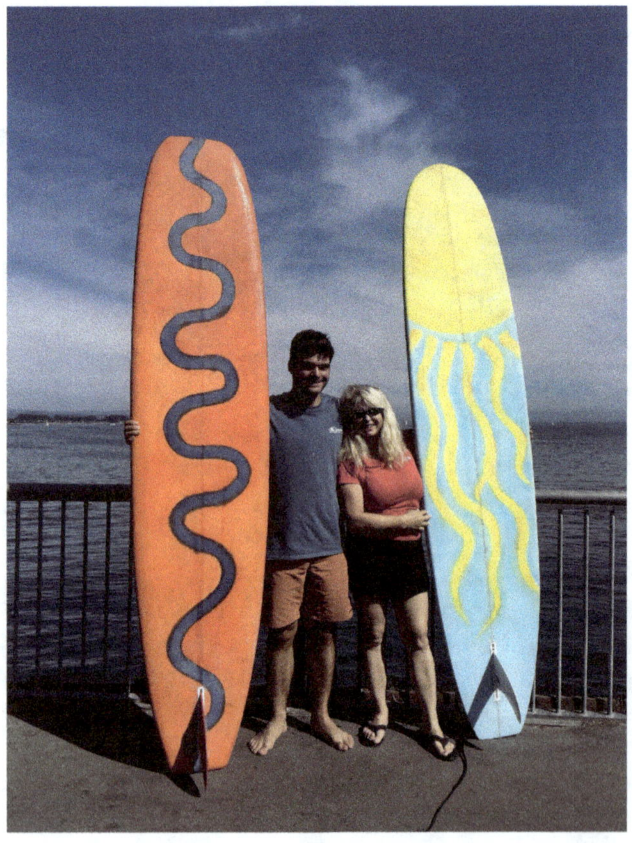

Fig. 11. Surf Day with the two surfboards Tommy shaped and glassed. Cowell's Cove, Santa Cruz, CA. Claudia Gray. *Surf Day*. 2019, collection of the artist.

I do want to mention that you don't have to be an amazing surfboard shaper, or a super technical artist to share community and create gifts. For instance, my children are great examples of this very thing. They all ebb and flow into different mediums. Olivia, loves to needlepoint and makes amazing projects that she gives to people as gifts. She also makes amazing fragrant soy candles for her friends and family. Liv also loves to draw and is becoming quite the little painter. Her style is much more technical and reminiscent of graphic artist or perhaps even tattoo artists, but nonetheless it's very creative and she's becoming quite talented. Alexandra, happens to be an excellent writer, editor and has written two plays that have been performed all before she became nineteen years old. She dabbles in a little knitting that Tommy showed her how to do and I have a very warm hat that she knitted me. Besides woodworking, surfboard shaping and knitting, Tommy also has fun silk-screening t-shirts. Jack loves metal shop at his high school and has created some wonderful projects. Among them are a beautiful metal butterfly that he twisted and welded for me. I display all their handmade gifts proudly as they make me feel happy and serene when I see all their creations. I feel the love they poured into their projects. The point I am trying to make, is that there is a special medium that may call to someone, but there is something for everyone. This includes all sorts of platforms, even perhaps even a computer coder that writes a poem in code for his beloved.

Community is also formed within art groups, fundraising art shows, and art coalitions. Examples are art leagues, art collectives and even art classes. Within many senior centers there is a camaraderie that is shared as the art teachers come teach the seniors artistic techniques that they can explore and keep their minds sharp.

There are also many active groups that get together such as plein air groups where painters share a beautiful landscape as they paint their own perspective on the scene in the outdoors. I belong to several of these magical groups. I have personally benefited from the locations that I may not have known of, the friendships, and the technical techniques and helpful criticism that was shared. After attending these art groups I often feel calm, happy and very satisfied that I came away with either a finished painting or something that just needed a little bit of studio work. Of course, not every session produced a fantastic piece of art, but what it did produce is a feeling of belonging and community with like-minded souls.

Through the creations of an artist, there is a community that is formed, acknowledged and revered. There is an art genre called community art. This is also known as community-engaged art, social art, community-based art, and sometimes dialogical art. This term has been used in the late 1960s as the practice grew in Canada, the USA and the United Kingdom, Ireland, the Netherlands, and Australia. The contributors of the *Tate* website describe it as, "Community art is artistic activity that is based in a community setting, characterized by interaction or dialogue with the community and often involving a professional artist collaborating with people who may not otherwise engage in the arts (Tate, para. 1).

Furthermore, this type of collaboration sometimes results in public installations in the community called public art which involve many people in the city. According to the Association for Public Art website, the contributor explain, "Public art is a reflection of how we see the world – the artist's response to our time and place combined with our own sense of who we are" (Association for Public Art, para. 1).

This helps different people come together involving a weaving of different talents:

> To some degree, every public art project is an interactive process involving artists, architects, design professionals, community residents, civic leaders, politicians, approval agencies, funding agencies, and construction teams. The challenge of this communal process is to enhance rather than limit the artist's involvement. (Association for Public Art, para. 2)

Another form of community art can also be seen in the every changing and growing internet. There are virtual communities and internet art has many forms. Of course, in performance arts, there are community theatre, community-engaged dance, and symphonies. There are numerous other types of creative community involvement. Additionally, artworks in these forms may include many types of media and characterized with interaction with the community. Virtual galleries have been a popular form of reaching audiences during COVID-19.

Lastly, there are the countless community exhibition where municipalities, companies, and organizations exhibit artwork. These events, including venues like wine and arts festivals bringing together the community for the sake of celebrating creativity. Good vibes are also felt in these celebrations. Kahar Zalmay wrote in *The News International:*

> Festivals have both social and economic angles. In the chaotic and stressful planet we inhabit, happiness is overshadowed by negativity and insecurity and so the need for something that could bring positivity has been felt time and again. Thus, festivals that give us the opportunity to forget all our worries and celebrate the positive side of life, even if it is for a few days, came into existence. (Zalmay)

# CHAPTER 5: CREATING PROFESSIONALLY

Circa 2012, my art would take a new turn of events. My creativity would turn from hobby and volunteerism to creating on a professional level. As I look back, I would have never said I would become a professional artist. Well, to be honest, most likely I would have said that sounds great! Where do I sign up? But I never really thought it would happen to me or that people would ever buy something I had made on a consistent basis.

It was 2012, and I was busy with my new glass experiments I was toying with. I found out about slumping glass from a recent trip to Pike Place Market in Washington. There, I learned that I would be able to continue helping the environment as I worked with glass. On that life changing trip, I learned that if you take a wine bottle that most likely would end up in the trash, place it in a kiln, you can then slump it. The end product can be a bowl or a flat bottle which you can use as a cheese board. Many of you may not have heard of this word, slumping, but it is a technical process. The *Bullseye Glass Company* website defines accordingly, "Slumping is a kilnforming process that uses heat and gravity to transform sheet glass into the shape of a mold. One can to create an almost endless variety of forms when slumping glass" (Bullseye, para. 3).

However, it's not as easy as it sounds, because glass is very tricky and it does not like to get too cold or too hot too fast. So the experiments I was working on was getting the right firing schedule and temperatures for my specific kiln. "When the glass is heated in a kiln and enters a liquid state, the force of gravity pulls it to the floor. In glass slumping, this 'floor' is some type of mold" (Bullseye). And if you happen to hold too hot of a temperature for too long, then you have a goopy glass mess at the bottom of your kiln. Now, in my mind, I go back to Pele, the Hawaiian fire goddess, and lava, which is almost what is happening as glass becomes molten and liquid.

I determined for my specific kiln it took six segment which I needed to perform manually. Because it did not have any automatic programming features like the newer kilns. I painstakingly set manual timers and change the temperature to the next cycle. I quickly found out that cooling the glass was as crucially important as heating it, otherwise it would crack:

> After the heated glass has flowed into the mold and assumed its shape, it is cooled back down to room temperature with an appropriate annealing phase. By the time the glass is fully returned to room temperature the liquid glass will be crystallized into the rigid form of glass with which we are most familiar. Its new permanent shape will be that of the mold. (Bullseye)

As I learned about glass, the idea of helping the environment somehow, all the while having fun with making art was fascinating to me. I have always had a special affinity to the environment, as I already had been published as a freelancer writer on environmental issues countless of times. Additionally, I had volunteered for the Sierra Club as a books editor. Helping the environment was something I can continue to do in the art world? Wait, this is becoming very motivational for me.

Over the years, I always had loved cooking and having fun dishes to serve my culinary creations. I was excited to see that with slumping, I could create one of a kind environmentally friendly dish-ware. Bullseye also agrees, as the website contributors state, "Slumping is a process that is commonly used to make food-bearing objects such as bowls and platters, but with some creativity one can create all kinds of interesting variations" (Bullseye).

I was also incorporating many environmental practices into my parenting with my own kids, and I was also trying to spread the word to others. I was one of the founding members of the Bee Green committee at their elementary school. That name was cute because the school's mascot was a bee. Also, I was the leader of two Cub Scout dens and two Girl Scout troops and my co-leaders and I would often plan field trips teaching kids and their families about the environment. I remember one such field trip where we went to the dump and they explained that glass actually takes 750 years to decompose in a landfill.

Shockingly, even though most municipalities recycle glass, often times commercial facilities, such as restaurants, do not recycle at all. Sometimes cities have what's called Dirty Murphy selection of trash where some of the recycling gets picked from the combined trash and moved to the recycling area. In any event, there was no guarantee that a bottle of wine, water or tea that is enjoyed would end up being recycled, most often they would just be thrown in the landfill and it would take 750 years to morph back into the earth. And we all know how popular wine is, and how many bottles are consumed annually. The numbers were staggering to me.

It was around this timeframe, when I was taking painting classes from a very talented artist, Sama Wareh, who also taught at the Newport Beach Environmental Center. The sessions were private and held at my home. I remember having so much fun exploring the different techniques I wanted to try. She would decipher what I wanted to work on and then she explained how it was done. I loved that I got to pick projects. I credit this teacher with showing me real fundamentals I was missing from my experience. We went over some basics also, reminders of how to hold a brush properly, how to mix paint, what size brushes to use, light and dark contrasts. She even shared with me her special artist secret of how white makes a huge difference on the highlights of a painting.

It was during one of these sessions that I told her about my glass experiments of my newfound idea of slumping glass into something purposeful like a cheeseboard (see fig. 12). I also told her about my used kiln that I purchased for $450 from a Craigslist ad. It came from a family that were selling the deceased grandma's art collection and supplies. She apparently made lots of different ceramic items and ceramic doll heads. With my teacher, I discussed how my kiln was old and it did not function 100%, and it did not have an electronic controller like the new ones. Because I wasn't sure if it was going to work with glass much, I didn't want to spend much on it.

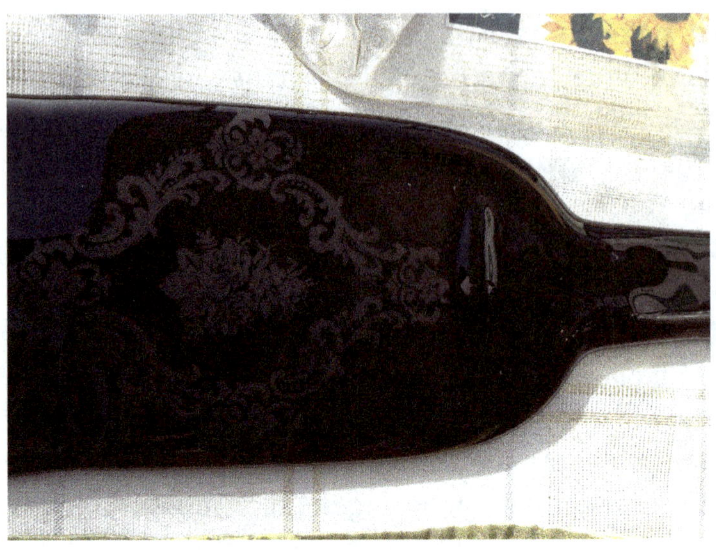

Fig. 12. One of my slumped bottles with an etching design. Claudia Gray. *Slumpy Etch*. 2012, collection of the artist.

I also showed her my other glass experiments where I was using used vases. Because I wanted to see how paint worked and how different colors mixed together, I was taking vases from thrift stores that I would purchase for like a dollar or two, and then I would create different painted versions of them. I would paint them with sponges, metallic paint, purple paint, brown, copper all sorts of different colors and used various techniques. They came out to be quite interesting because in painting what seemed to be hundreds of vases, it taught me not be afraid of using paint or new techniques. In a way, I was teaching myself to just have fun with the art, experiment with different tools, sponges, brushes, paper towels, etc. Without actually knowing what I was doing, I was probably training myself to work fast, with fun in mind, and without fear. After all, I thought, not much is invested as this was just a vase that cost me two dollars.

She listened and held the vases and cheeseboards in her hands. I could see her brain gears moving, as she said something like, "I think you're ready for your first art show, and the center is having one in May. Do you think you can bring some of your recycled glass cheese boards and some of the other items and do you want to sell at it?" She really loved the idea that it was ecofriendly which fit in perfectly with the Environmental Nature Center's purpose. I was flabbergasted and so excited, as I never thought I would be in an art show and people actually buying my art (see fig. 13). I really owe

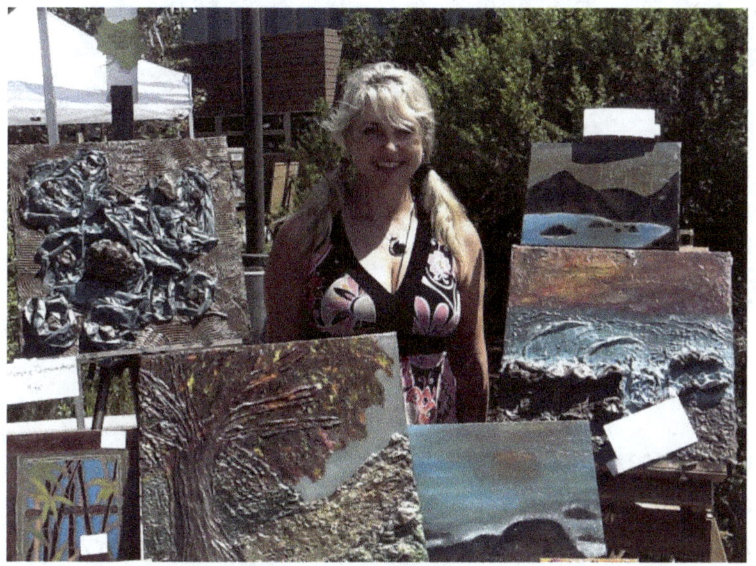

Fig. 13. Environmental Nature Center Show, May 2012. Claudia Gray. *First Show.* 2012, collection of the artist.

her quite a bit because she started me on this journey
At my first art show, I really brought way too much stuff, this was so exciting for me to be able to bring things. And did I really need to bring all the vases that I had worked on, probably not. But I spread out and there was a smile on my face, my wares were on display and for sell. Surprisingly, I

actually made quite a few sales that day and definitely more than I had thought. Some of my vases sold, some of my first paintings sold, and even some of these glass bottle cheeseboards sold (see fig. 14). Because my items were

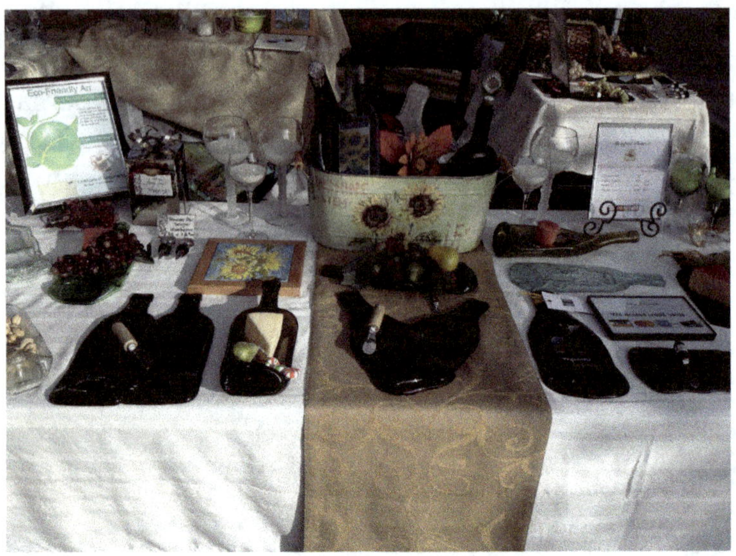

Fig. 14. Samples of my slumped bottle cheese trays and bowls. Claudia Gray. *Bottle Display.* 2013, collection of artist.

recycled, they fit in perfectly into this environmental nature themed show. But here's what happened as I got hooked. I couldn't believe that people actually wanted to buy my items. Which is an interesting because if I think back, I have many times throughout my life sold things that I made. This goes back to when I was in fourth grade. In contemplation of my years, I think I have always been a maker.

Here's what I remember when I was in fourth grade that was probably the very first time I sold my art creations. So my parents were from modest income, they were immigrants from Argentina and so we frequented garage sales and many times people just gave us stuff. I don't know exactly where I got a Snoopy spirograph, but it was amazing. I had so much fun putting the different gears together and using colored pens to draw the peanuts characters without actually being able to draw!

My friends looked at it and would say wow that's really cool. So my fellow students and I were really into reading. At some point, I realized hey why don't I make little book markers out of these cute little Peanuts characters. So I did and I would sell them for five cents each. So technically, it was here, in fourth grade that it was the first time I put one of my creations out in the market. And surprisingly my fellow students bought them up. Of course, this was not a scalable market, I now chuckle. I mean, I could have gone into the other fourth grade room or the third graders or perhaps the sixth grade rooms, but I was just happy selling them to my class.

In any event, the Peanuts book marker phase quickly passed, but somehow it was lodged into my long-term memory. I do have a very clear understanding of what happened. This might have been the very beginning of me making something that I thought could sell. And in creative terms, would be to listen to an inspiration, act on it and give it form. Then sell it to a market that values the object presented.

Although I did not have formal art classes, I still had a need to create. There are clear examples of this in my teenage years. In high school, I founded the Balloons Afloat company that sold helium balloons and created balloon bouquets. My friend and I developed it and it was quite popular for a while.

Fast forward to when I was approximately eighteen years old, I had a very dear friend, who is still one of my buddies, and we would make handmade photo albums. She got my creativity going again somehow with these cloth and lace super decked out albums. Somehow, I never really had the opportunity to go to art school. The only art class I had at that time was in high school, and if I looked back at my drawings they weren't half bad. They might help have been the best in the class but they certainly weren't the worst. I remember being very happy being in that class and so excited to go to it and I would focus so much on my drawings. But, I was going to be a business major in college and so yeah, art is for kids that can have fun, my brain said. I needed to study business so I can be successful. So I thought. Perhaps a bit of the 80s yuppy mentality had a hold of me.

In contemplation of the past, I think I was misaligned with my true passions, and was not afforded the opportunity to follow them. Probably because I did not have any formal training and I didn't think I would do very well at it. After all, what did I have to show as part of my portfolio, Snoopy book-markers? Balloons? Moreover, I continued to think that artists didn't make money. Consequently, I was going to be a business major in undergraduate school just to make sure I could support myself.

Foreshadowing to the future, that major didn't last long and I realized that my mind didn't really work that way. As a junior, I switched over to psychology as my major. I then graduated and worked in an outside sales position, which was a natural thing for me, since I sold cosmetics for many years when I was 16 years old for Estée Lauder and Lancôme. I eventually left the employee benefits sales position and went into human resources for six years which actually combined the psychology and the business education I had received. All these experiences helped in creating my company, being a sales person at art shows, etc. But I digress… ok back to me being a maker.

Around my early twenties, I started to paint watercolor and took some casual classes. I was fascinated with how colors blended into other colors. I had a lot of fun with experimenting with the different ways to make paint synthesize with other colors. Then at some point, I thought wait, if I cut up these colorful pieces, then I could make watercolor paper earrings. I had never seen such a thing, but apparently they existed. So I went to a shop, and bought the metal backings for the earrings and the special glue required. These earrings were my first jewelry creations. I gave these away during the holidays or to friends. I didn't really sell them, but I could see that my brain was moving in that direction.

Then more fast forwarding to my late twenties, I start to want to create things again. Somewhere along the line, I had more time and I wanted to satisfy this yearning that was ever present in the back of my mind. I couldn’t understand why I wanted to make things, but I did. One of my friends then hires me to make her curtains for her bedroom. She told me what she wanted and she picked the fabric and color. Frankly, they were the most hideous avocado color curtains ever, which her husband even said so. But he couldn’t blame that on me as she was the one that picked the color. Overall, I did an ok job sewing. However, you could definitely tell that they were not professionally produced, but that started me making things again.

It was during this period that I started to sew more often. I was thinking one day, while in the fabric part of a superstore that there are a lot of remnants in this store. What could I do with all this extra fabric that people don't want? For whatever reason, I am all for making things out of nothing, or scraps, something that someone's going to throw away. Why? I have no idea really.

I pondered the issue and I came up with I hate when hair gets in my eyes when I exercise. So, I decided to make scrunchies. During this timeframe, it was still a time when scrunchies were in fashion. So I made about five billion of them, no just kidding, probably quite a few hundred. I gave them to everybody and I just gave them away. I even made cute labels that I would print and attach to the product. I called the brand "Living Well."

Pretty labels, and all, I still really had no market for them. After all, how could you sell something like that without a venue. This problem, is what may have help to create the eBays and the Etsys of the world. However, during that time frame, there were none of these markets. Funny without a marketplace, things get created and don't flow out to the world very easily. Consequently, I think I might still have a huge bag of them in my garage.

A little funny note about how these scrunchies still live on, is that my kids at one point saw these scrunchies, and I do have two girls and I gave them a few scrunchies. Even though they were not in style they took them and said something like, "Aw thanks, you made these, cool Mom. They are retro." And, so with the ones I gave my daughters, there are less scrunchies in my garage.

In reflection, probably sewing was role modeled for me as I remember thinking back when I was in Argentina watching my Godmother sew thousands of cloth napkins. I mean, I had never seen so many napkins in all of my life. She must have had some sort of commercial job to create all the napkins for the whole world. As I was young, it seemed like these napkins were stacked up high as she would sew them with ease and speed.

Probably, if I contemplate this further, she might have put in the seed into my brain that a woman can create something, have it be beautiful and purposeful and it in turn can provide money somehow. Now, that I think about this further, I do have to give her credit for my inspiration to create these early works of mine on a sewing machine.

It was around this scrunchies period in the late 1990s timeframe that I was getting treatment for a double hand injury at very well known local university hand clinic. There, they were using paraffin wax on my hands. Although the treatment felt really good, I was noticing how much wax was being thrown out. This was outrageous as I was thinking about the environment. I was wondering why all this wax is being produced. And is it being thrown into the landfill just after only one use? So I had a new found inspiration. I then started to research what can be made with wax. It then occurred to me…candles!

It was also during this time that I was an avid hiker about 4 to 5 times a week. And quite often there were beautiful wildflowers in bloom. I didn't take too many, just enough to press and dry them. I then asked my hand therapist if I could have some extra wax that was being thrown out anyway. He said yes, and then "Living Well" candles was born.

I researched and figured out how to make candles. There was no internet or youTube back then, so this was a little more challenging than nowadays. Still environmentally inspired, I even made the candles out of throwaway jars that I cleaned very well. The beautiful pressed flowers were placed between the reused jar and wax showing their beauty through the clear glass. In reflection, somehow I was out to save all the trash from the world! I guess… apparently, an important form of inspiration and concern was to somehow repurpose things into useful objects of beauty and purpose.

These candles did sell very well because pretty wild flowers, recycled wax and I even added some fragrances to them. I found a way to sell them at the frequent garage sales my friend and I were having at her place. Yes, she was still speaking to me, albeit her husband hated the avocado green curtains. We would always laugh about this, and she would say that she loved that color and that's why she chose it. These statements, got me thinking that art is subjective. One person can love, let's say a certain color or texture and another one would be repulsed by it.

This subjectivity in the arts thinking was early training for me with regard to not taking it personally if someone does not like your artwork. In looking ahead, to the future, I would encounter subjectivity time and time again at various art venues.

Although the candles were selling, I still could not sell enough to really make a big profit because the only place they were being marketed was at our garage sales. Again, there was no easy to use online market like, Etsy, Facebook Marketplace, Instagram, or eBay in existence yet or at least that I knew about. And, it is hard to believe, and I might be dating myself, but the Internet was there, but it wasn't taking off yet, this was the late 1990s. The world was different then and much more difficult to sell items.

Two of my favorite memories about these candles were about product liability and using correct materials for the product. These are things that you might not learn about unless you make mistakes, like I did. So here's what happened, I remember one of the sweetest stories of my candles being purchased is by a gentleman. He wanted to give to his wife that had just given birth to their new baby. I was really touched and I thought this is a wonderful thing to be able to create something that someone values enough to gift on such a cherished event. Definitely, I had amazing positive feelings about that.

The second clear memory about these candles, took place during a house space clearing where I had my church people come over to my newly purchased home. So we were going around the house saying prayers, and then all of a sudden someone says, “Oh my gosh, the curtain might be catching on fire!” Apparently, one of my candle wicks started to really burn higher than it should've and I mistakenly had the candle too close by the cloth curtain. My first thought, was glad we are blessing this home as this could be is the Amityville Horror house.

I quickly put out the candle and there was not an actual fire. In the next days following the incident, I would troubleshoot if I had policies or ideas in place in terms of product liability. And how did this particular candle burn the way it did? I also thought about what might be happening with people that already bought candles from me? Should I have put some sort of use at your own risk disclaimer on the jars? And then… I thought about the poor gentleman’s newborn baby that might be catching on fire. Ok, that didn't really happen, it was just my imagination going wild.

In my mind, I would reflect and decipher the malfunction. I then realized that it could have been from using cotton twine instead of commercial wicks. Additionally, I then learned that paraffin wax is made from petroleum, consequently it does not burn clean. All this became more clear a couple of decades later when I started to make my professional candles circa 2012.

Unlike back in the 1990s, now I had a venue to market them as they were being sold at various art shows. Learning from my past mistake, I wanted things to burn clean, so primarily I only made them out of soy. At times, I would melt down old candles and reuse the wax, but I did not like the fumes I was being exposed to, so I only rarely made these recycled wax types. Another signature designer element to my soy candles, was I was reusing beautiful china cups, tea sets, and glassware, thereby making each of them a one of a kind candles (see fig. 15).

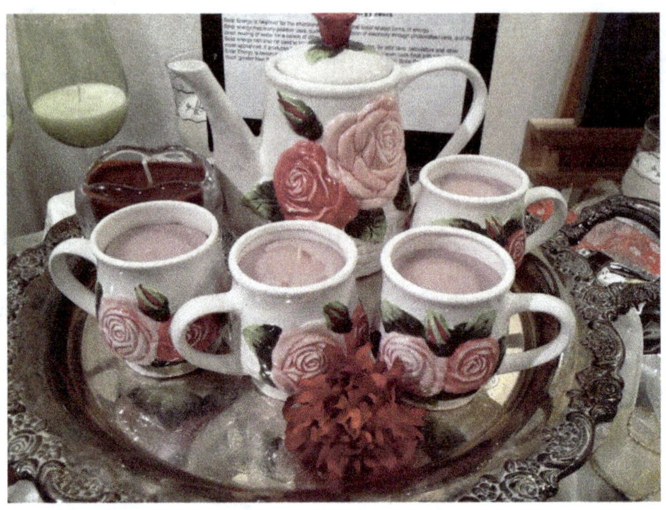

Fig. 15. One of my tea set candles. Claudia Gray. *Tea Set Candles*. 2012, collection of the artist.

Although I was producing hundreds of these candles (see fig. 16), this time around, I was more business savvy and I put disclaimer labels on the bottom, as most companies did that as commonplace. During one of my creative sessions, my anxiety must have gotten a hold of me because I started to go down a rabbit home of remembering that that poor family of almost twenty years ago purchased one of my candles that was not burning clean. I was mortified and I hope that baby, probably now a twenty-something is OK and does he have lung breathing issues? Or maybe the candle sat unburned as the wild flowers were so pretty that they dare not burn it. All these what if scenarios my mind created were not helpful, and I will never know what really happened anyway.

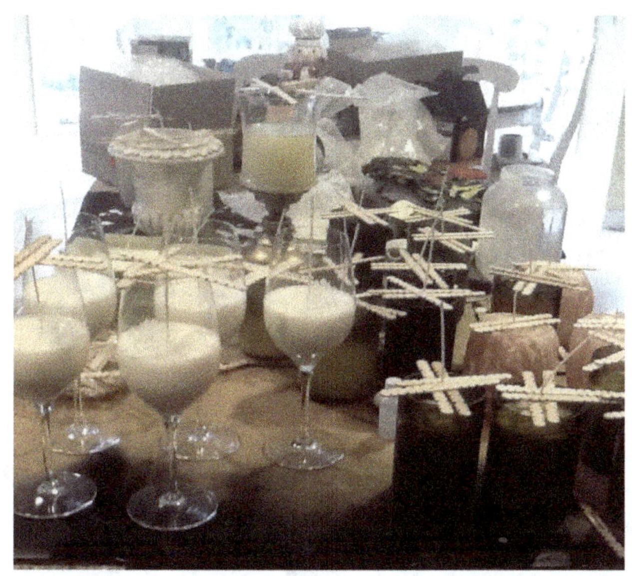

Fig. 16. My kitchen was transformed into a candle shop. Claudia Gray. *Candle Shop.* 2012, collection of the artist.

Although my rumination of the family and my paraffin candle was not useful, it did provide me with the seed thought on non-attachment for my creations. For instance, how was it that I was still remembering this family over 20 years later? It was probably because I was so excited to have sold one of my products to them and it was one of my first professional items I made. I felt very responsible for it and it was very early in my selling things journey. However, what I realized was if I make something, I have to let it go. It will go to the right person. I will try to make everything safe and follow guidelines. And I tried to believe when it goes to someone's house it is theirs. I am done with it. Because can you imagine me ruminating over the hundreds and hundreds of items I have sold? It would be impossible and it cannot be good for my mind. So this family also served the purpose of helping me start letting go of my creations.

I know this ideal is a difficult concept for some artists, but that has been my philosophy. It wasn't easy at first, but I realized that my real gift is the creative flow that I experience while I create the object. I also love seeing people feel happy when they buy my creations which is positive reinforcement to let go of those items.

Sure, there are some artwork pieces that are very special and I don't want to sell them. These might be one of kind first pieces where I explored a technique and finally got it. For ones I want to keep or pass on to my kids at some point, those become part of my private collection. I also heard from one of my teachers that it is really great to have art from each of your eras and phases that you created. I agree with this practice, and I have kept perhaps one or two items from each of my chapters. This method also shows a history of the art career and the growth.

Moreover, what I learned as an artist, was to actually have non-attachment to my creations. I was starting to understand that creativity flows through me. I make form out of something, but then I let it go. Then the object goes to the right person or to the right house. Sometimes when I create a special necklace or art piece I often wonder whom I am making this for and who will eventually wear it. Jessica Libor in her article entitled, "How to Practice Non-Attachment While Still Goal Setting in Your Art Career" elaborates on this point:

> If you create from the mindset of a gift, of doing your absolute and passionate best and caring your deepest and releasing that to the world, then you can be certain that if it didn't work out, it was because of things beyond your control. And you can practice non-attachment to those things outside your control, which makes life a whole lot more peaceful! (Libor, para. 17)

Along those lines, just because you are practicing non-attachment does not mean that you get to put unsafe products into the marketplace. Libor explains:

> Non attachment is NOT about floating through the world avoiding responsibility or trying to avoid caring about anything. That is actually not healthy and is more about trying to shield yourself from any hurt by not letting anything matter to you. This is not what the heart of non attachment is talking about. (Libor, para. 5)

Admitting, I was beginning to practice non-attachment to my artwork, but I still had the liability issue with the candles.

In the end a couple years later around 2016 or so, I stopped making candles because insurance for candle makers became ridiculously expensive. As I was required to hold insurance for the art shows, I did not feel like they were profitable enough to continue to make them. This insurance issue came about because apparently people did not make the candles correctly, and users sometimes left the candles unattended, therefore, house fires were happening left and right. My insurance agent told me that even though the candles were being burned unattended, claims were being placed against the candle maker. My current insurance carrier did not even cover candles as a product although they had covered me for years and I did not have any claims against me.

Nevertheless, this particular year, they required that I sign a candle disclaimer that I would not make any candles. I decided to not pursue candle making and concluded that from the current marketplace, insurance claims and so on, candles were no longer safe nor profitable for me to make. So my muses pointed me to another medium and I left candle making to others willing to take out expensive insurance out with product liability. I still had one burning question, why would people leave the candles unattended anyway? Maybe they fall asleep because the fragrance and the aroma are just so relaxing? Again, a rabbit hole not worth pursuing.

As I continued to play, explore and create, I was making all sorts of new creations. My small little art business was mushrooming. Part of me was feeling a little hooked on creating art to sell. As a long-time stay home mom, which is truly the best job I ever had, my kids were getting older, and although I continued to volunteer quite a bit in their school, scouting and activities, they were becoming teenagers. At one point, my older children asked if I can maybe do my own thing and volunteer less. I understood what my older kids were saying, they needed to start the individualization process that all teenagers go through. And so they encouraged my art hobby. Simultaneously, the universe and muses were somehow propelling my artwork into the market. By the end of 2012, my company, Gray Designs (yes, I know, another identity) was becoming its own brand. By December of that same year, after many more arts and crafts shows, I exhibited in a major juried art show at the Los Angeles convention center.

In summary, my art was accepted into the marketplace as I continued to sell at juried arts and wine shows, galleries, wholesale shows and at the height of my production, at thirty-five retail stores (see fig. 17). I believe the main reason was each of the items I made were one of a kind. At this stage, I was experimenting and I often used new techniques all the time, thereby making each bottle or art piece unique. My studio grew and I owned three kilns, all with nifty automatic electronic controllers. I even produced 450 pieces for a major hotel in Southern California. Two hundred of my custom surfboards were being used for serving their sliders, and two

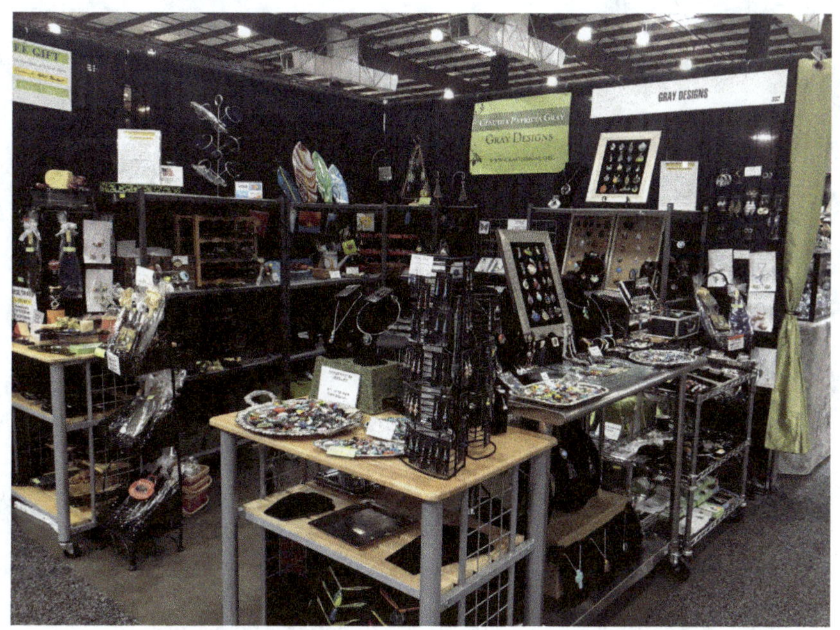


Fig. 17. One of my large convention show booths. Claudia Gray. *Convention Booth. 2015*, collection of the artist.

hundred and fifty glass plates were being used for their high-tea service. It all worked out great for about eight years, until life turned upside down. With the family changes, economic circumstances and the COVID-19 pandemic in full swing, decisions had to be made. My beloved studio in the redwood forest was, unfortunately, closed in 2021 (see fig. 18).

However, that is not the end of my artistic story, as I am still creating and trekking on this journey. Perhaps my next actual studio will be just as grand, or maybe smaller but more creative. I do not know the answers yet. However, I am certain my Muses are working on all these details. I can't wait to see what they come up with for me.

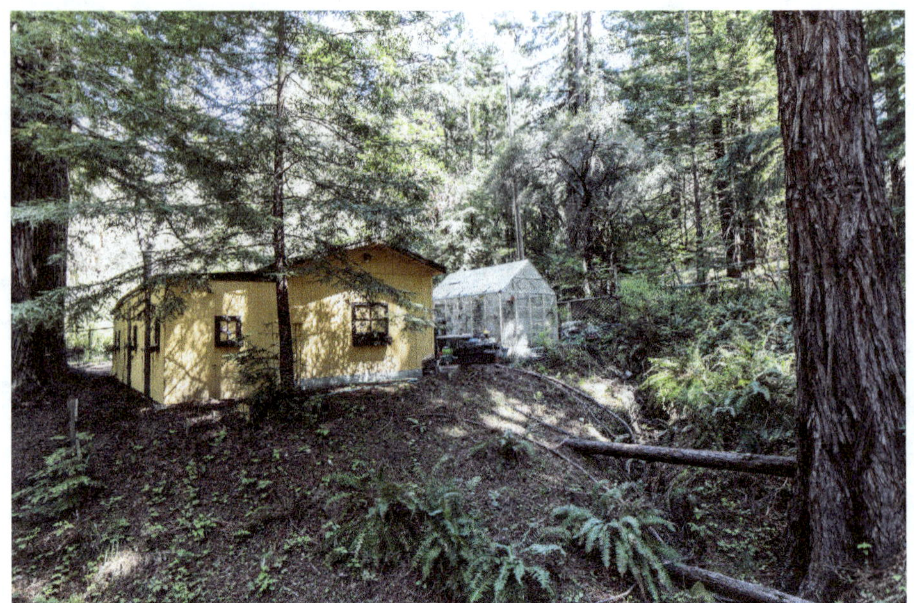

Fig. 18. My beloved redwood forest studio in the Santa Cruz Mountains. Claudia Gray. *Redwood Studio*. 2021, collection of the artist.

# CHAPTER 6: CREATING FROM PASSION

One thing that I noticed early on was that even though students are in a classroom working on the same project, each individual is fueled by their own inspiration. For some, it may be airplanes, or boats, for me it was surfboards and dragonflies for a while. Currently, I cannot stop painting waterlilies, just like my beloved and ever inspirational favorite artist, Claude Monet. Emile Zola, a French novelist, playwright, and journalist who is best-known for his contributions to the literary school of naturalism and to the development of theatrical naturalism, once said, "I would rather die of passion than boredom,"

Creating what is near and dear to your heart is easy and comes naturally. I can completely emerge myself in the shapes, colors and ideals behind the objects I am creating.

Finding your passion is important as you do anything in life, whether you are creating artwork or working in the tech world. Sometimes, what you need to create is very simple, it makes sense to create that object. This quote from Steve Jobs illustrates what I am talking about, “Creativity is just connecting things. When you ask creative people how they did something, they feel a little guilty because they didn’t really do it, they just saw something. It seemed obvious to them after a while” (Johnson).

And so, if you create from what you know and hold dear, it may become more effortless if let’s say you created something that held no interest to you. According to the *Indeed* website’s Editorial Team, in an article entitled "8 Ways To Find Your Passion,” they write, “When you discover something you're passionate about, you gain a purpose. Passions drive you to excel and motivate you to learn. If you're excited to pursue certain activities and interests, you grow your abilities with a specific focus” (Indeed).

When I enrolled in my first fused glass art class around 2013, the instructor asked each of us to come up with a project that we wanted to create and design. I was very quick to come up with my answer, it must have taken about two whole seconds - SURFBOARDS! When it was my turn to explain what I was going to create, the teacher mentioned that he had never seen one of these in glass and that there may be issues with the curvature of the Surfboard design and shape. So we discussed some of the elements that I needed to understand and issues I needed to solve. I remember, when I created my first Surfboard, I was so happy. And it turned out pretty OK. I called it, “Surfs Up.” I brought it to one of my local art organization for the monthly showing and it ended up winning the popular choice award ribbon.

I went on to make many more surfboards (see fig. 19). I would make them for decorative purposes, but because glass is food safe, I decorated them at my art shows with a cute little cheese knife, and perhaps some fake food on top of it. Then they started to sell as decorative plates. At one point, I had them advertised on my website. That turned out to be one of the best decisions I made regarding this creation, as this was how a major Southern California hotel contacted me.

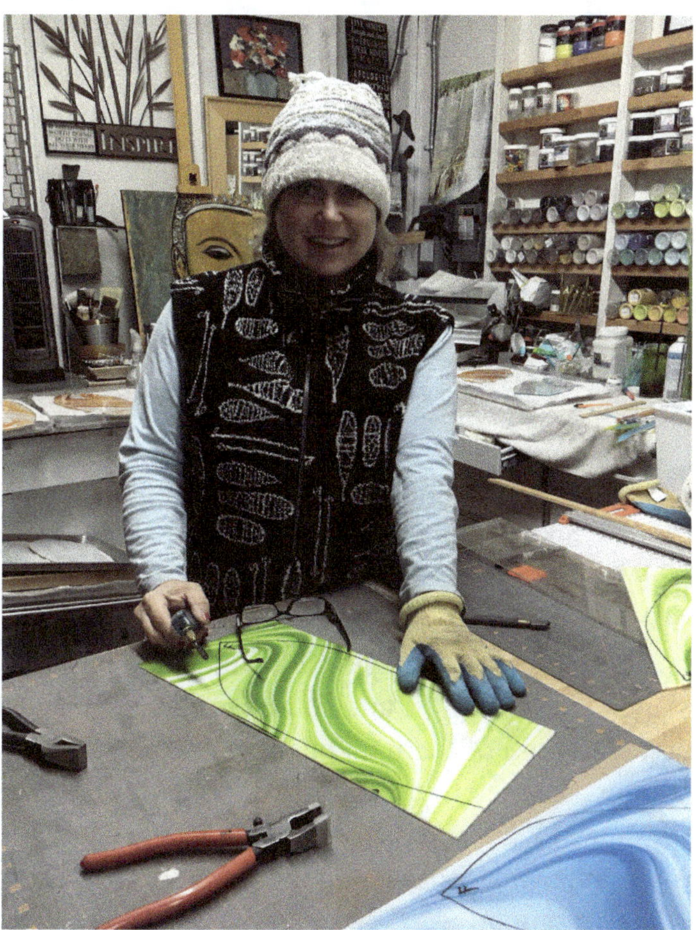

Fig. 19. In my studio, where I am happily cutting glass surfboards. Olivia Gray. *Cutting Glass*. 2015, collection of the artist.

The hotel buyer said that the new chef from Hawaii was moving over to their hotel and he was interested in serving sliders on surfboards. Hence, they were looking for surfboard plates. However, they could not find them anywhere in shops, and so they were exploring the Internet and found me. I ended up making two hundred surfboard platters for this hotel chain and an additional two hundred and fifty glass plates for their high tea service. This proved to be my biggest order ever and it all stemmed from my passion years before when I wanted to create a surfboard at my glass class.

But surfboards are not my only passion. In my both my photography and glasswork I seemed to be obsessed with showcasing dragonflies. Somehow when I was hiking through nature or on a photo shoot, these magnificent little creatures would hover near me. At some point, I took notice of how often I was encountering them in such varied locations. I started to photograph them.

I did not know what the dragonfly significance was, until one time in my studio I was pondering why I was putting dragonflies into most things I was making. There must be a reason why I keep encountering them and why I want to place them in my art. And when I say most designs, I mean, I placed dragonflies, on glass platters, ornaments, sun-catchers, slumped bottles, necklace pendants in various designs and sizes, earrings, and so on (see fig. 20). I just couldn't get enough of them and neither could my clientele. My customers seemed to devour them as fast as I could make them (see fig. 21). So one day, I decided to see what all this dragonfly mania was about. With a quick internet search, I had an "aha" moment.

As it turns out, and congruent with the events happening in my life at the time, the Dragonfly spiritual totem

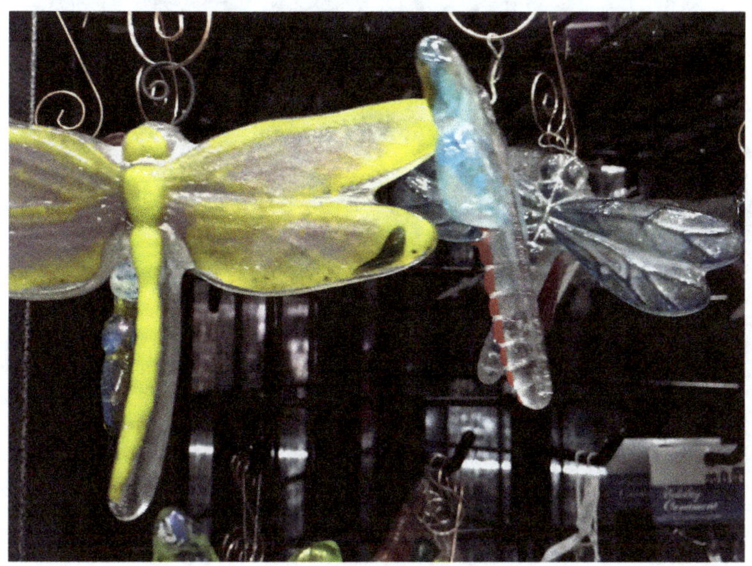

Fig. 20. Samples of my dragonfly ornaments. Claudia Gray. *Dragonfly Ornaments*. 2015, collection of the artist.

is for transformation and wisdom. Elena Harris, author of the article entitled, *Dragonfly Spirit Animal & Totem,* writes:

> As it turns out Dragonflies start to grow in water and then move into the air and fly. When this spirit animal shows up in your life you may be called to transform and evolve. Symbol of metamorphosis and transformation, it inspires those who have it as a totem to bring about the changes needed in their lives in order to go to reach their full potential. When this spirit animal shows up in your life, it's an indication that it's time for change. Just like the dragonfly changes colors as it matures, you may be called to live and experience yourself differently. Stay open to the enfoldment of your personal journey. (Harris)

Wow, I thought. How interesting that I had a fascination for dragon flies and they started to appear, or perhaps I merely noticed them more. But either way, it did not

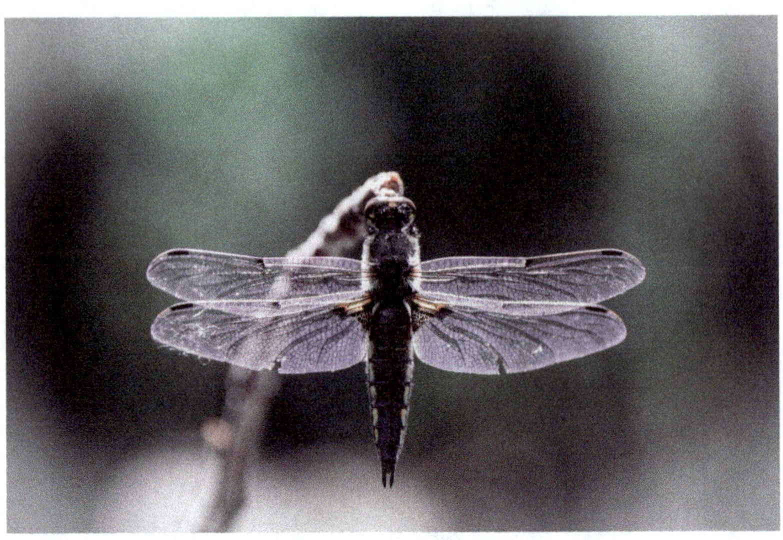

Fig. 22. Claudia Gray. *Madame Dragonfly.* 2016, collection of the artist.

matter. They were around me, and I took notice. As Henry David Thoreau says, "It's not what you look at that matters, it's what you see" (Johnson). Albeit, I was encountering them, but I also had a need and craving to create form out of them via glass, photography and jewelry. I also made photography products, such as metal prints, canvas print and greeting cards. Here's one of my best selling dragon fly shots (see fig. 22).

The enchanting Ms. Madame dragonfly, was not the only spiritual photographic encounter I had. In fact, I was happily learning that there are many colors of dragonflies. Hence, when a different variety of dragon fly appeared, I took note. Once on a zoo field trip, I was greeted by a red dragonfly. I remember, we shared many moments together as I tried to get just the right angle. Luckily, as in the past, this dragon fly complied and collaborated with me to pose just perfectly with the type of background I was going with.

I was also intrigued to know that the Japanese consider red dragon flies to be extremely sacred. They believe that they are a symbol of strength, courage and happiness. The Native Americans also hold red dragon flies in high regard as they can oftentimes show a time of rejuvenation after much hardship. Which serendipitously, also paralleled by life, although I had not realized it at that moment of time (see fig. 23).

Understanding why I was putting form to these insects and creating art out of them I understood my transformation and my growth as a person. But why did my clients keep buying them as fast as I could make the artwork? I started to ask the question to people that picked up a dragonfly and said do you know what the dragonfly symbolizes? Sometimes they they would say yes and then explain that they needed to have it for themselves or for a friend that's going through a massive change.

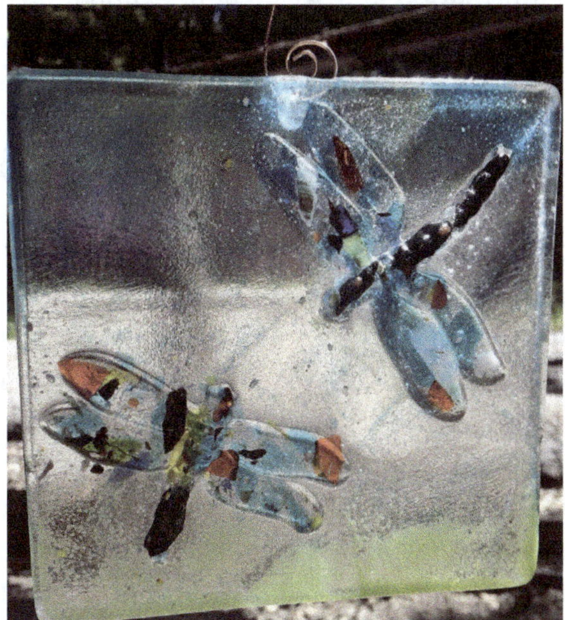

Fig. 21. One of my dragonfly sun catchers. Claudia Gray. *Dragonfly Sun Catcher.* 2015, collection of the artist.

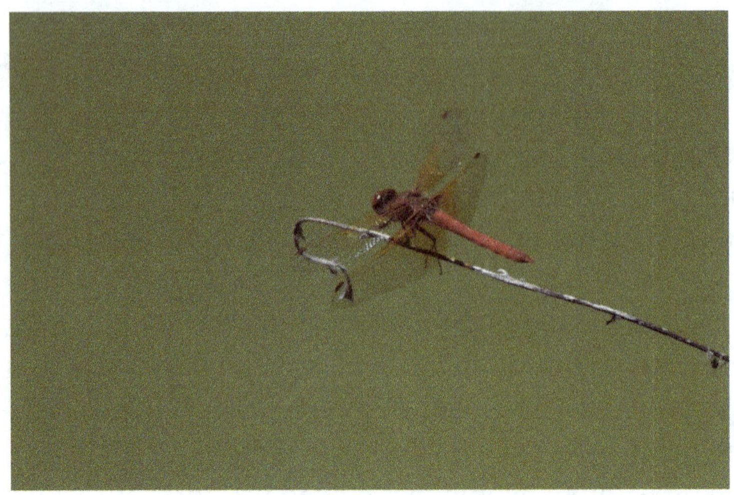

Fig. 23. Claudia Gray. *Red Dragonfly.* 2016, collection of the artist.

Other times they would say no, and I would ask them if they wanted to understand. Approximately 99% of the time they said sure explain it to me, and I would say it was a symbol of transformation and wise change, and a positive evolvement. Then remarkably, again about 99% of the time they would say oh that makes so much sense. I have to have this now. I am going through this massive blah blah blah, or my friend is going through some sort of cancer treatment or other sorts of different life altering situations.

Somehow, I intuitively knew that creativity was flowing through me as it appeared I was a conduit for not only my own change in my life's growth, but for other people and their friends and family. I was creating artwork that somehow was soothing for them and would help them through their respective transformations. Perhaps it was just the little something that gave them a positive vibe during their day and helped with the challenges they were encountering.

But not everything I created was about internal changes and metamorphosis. I also get inspired by things that are meaningful for me like waves. As a surfer and someone that grew up swimming in the Southern California swells, I loved everything about the subject matter. The colors of waves are interesting and the shapes are ever changing. Not only did I create waves as glass sculptures, but I also loved to paint them (see fig. 24). I might paint them focusing on their tubular shape or perhaps gentling rolling in the beaches.

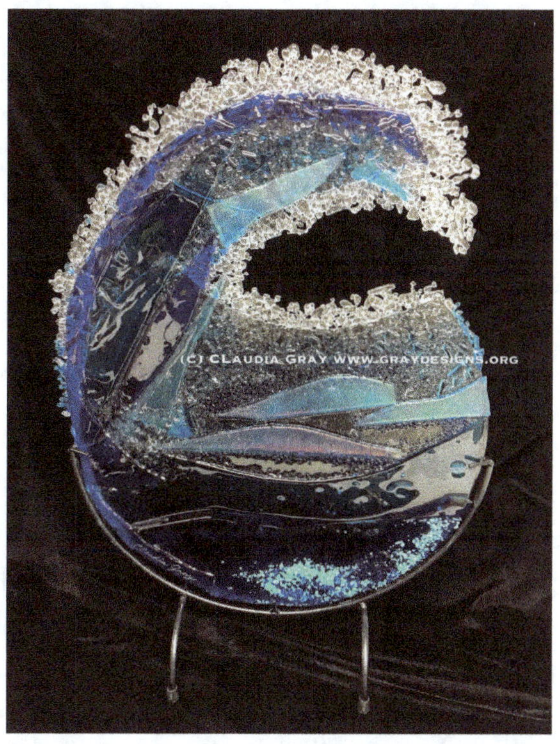


Fig. 24. Claudia Gray. *Glass Wave Sculpture*. 2017, collection of the artist.

Another fascination of mine has long been Hawaii. In one of my favorite life chapters, I was lucky to live on the island of Oahu in the town of Kailua for almost two years. I remember always being fascinated by Hawaiian culture, the scenery and especially hula. When I graduated from undergrad university, I chose Hawaii to celebrated. From there on, I was in love and curious about learning more about all the islands and culture. When moving back coming back to the mainland, it seemed like Hawaiian sirens kept calling me. I visited Hawaii many times and explored the majority of the islands.

Polynesian cultural items I was mesmerized with included the gods and how they were responsible for certain things happening on the islands. Pele, the goddess of fire and volcanoes is believed to be the creator of the Hawaiian islands. According to the *National Park Service* website, the contributors state, “Pele is the Hawaiian volcano deity, an elemental force, and the creator of these volcanic landscapes. According to tradition, she is embodied by the lava and natural forces associated with volcanic eruptions” (National Park Service).

I felt a kinship for Pele ever since I could remember, but even more so because as a fused glass artist I am working with really hot kilns, and transforming hard glass into liquid magma so to speak. I wanted to pay tribute to Pele in a glass sculpture. I set out to try some new techniques that I was experimenting with and ended up making,“Molten Magma” a twelve inch round glass sculpture paying tribute to the Hawaii, the volcanic forces that create new earth, and Pele (see fig. 25). On my website, I wrote the following description for the sold piece that I donated to a school fundraiser gala:

> Inspired by a recent trip to the Hawaii Volcanoes National Park, “Molten Magma” is a depiction of smelted rock residing beneath the Earth. Magma (from the Greek word μάγμα, "thick unguent") is a mixture of liquefied or semi-molten rock. Besides igneous rock, magma may also contain suspended crystals, dissolved gas and sometimes gas bubbles. This piece has been kiln fired three times to achieve an

artistic representation of the flowing red hot magma. Because this work of art is circular and the signature is on the backside, one can rotate the sculpture and display it differently. The Artist has etched intended proposed "top" and "bottom," on the back, but welcomes fluid movement of sculpture just as magma is ever moving and changing. (Gray)

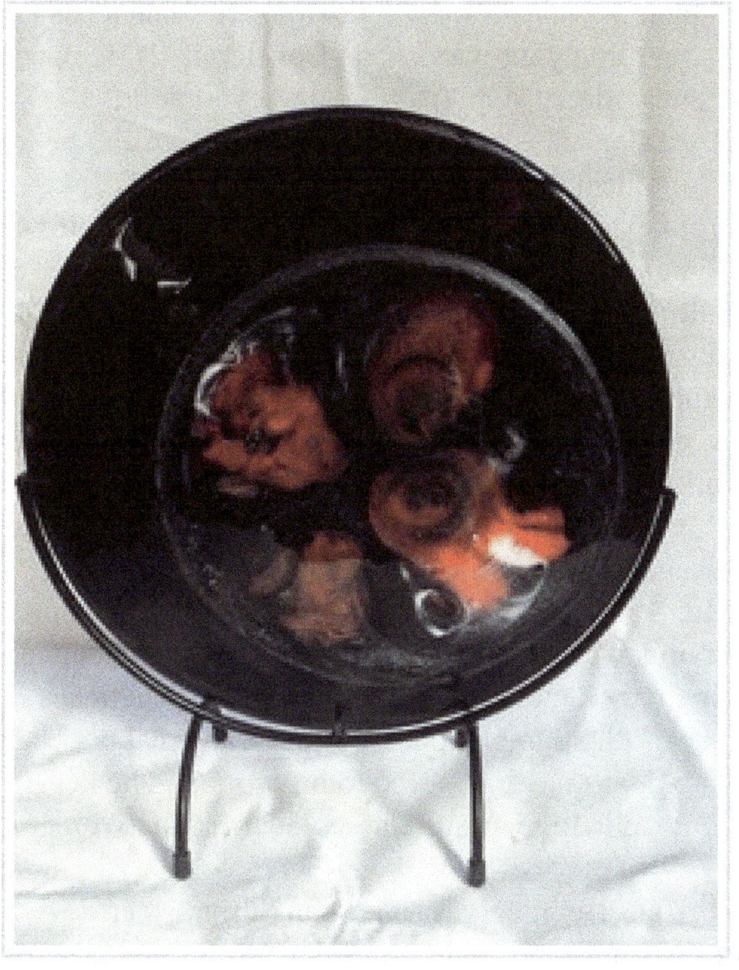

Fig. 25. Claudia Gray. *Molten Magma*. 2015, collection of the artist.

So if it is easier to create things you love, how do you find your passion and express it in art? There's lots of ways. You just have listen to yourself and think of the things you like to do and what makes you happy. According to the *Indeed* website, they include the following ways how to find passion. They write:

> Discovering what you're passionate about can shape who you are and what you will become both on the job and in your personal life. Here are some ideas to help you find your passion: 1) Develop it, 2) Be open to new ideas, 3) Put passion into everything, 4) Consume more ideas, 5) Slow down and be in the moment, 6) Make having fun the goal, 7) Take classes to explore your passions, and 8) Ask yourself what's next. (Indeed)

And ultimately, if you are having fun creating it, people will pick up on that vibe. Likewise, if you are passionate about something in a negative way or emotionally repressing some urges, people will also feel those as they view or pick up your artwork.

I believe this is just the case when the viewer receives a message from an artist, and that message can be a little twisted. As we all know, art sometimes just isn't all pretty with rainbows and unicorns. There are artists that have become very famous just for expressing their fetiches. In a History of Photography course I first learned about Hans Bellmer. I was never exposed to his work and he kept showing up in my various classes, such as, the Women in Art Class.

Hans Bellmer was a German Surrealist artist living from 1902 until 1975. He is best known for his life-sized pubescent female dolls he created in the mid-1930s. Not only did he make the dolls, but he photographed them in sexually provocative, unconventional poses, and mutated forms. Albeit he is not a woman, he made a career out of his blatant objectification of women. Not only were his images sexualizing women, but his images included dolls that he purposefully made with a creepy and violent flavor. His artwork seemed to portray internal demons he was dealing with and managed to conceptualize in his artwork. As critics most would agree, that his work was full of dark feeling and unfulfilled sexual desire.

I often thought about how he did create things he was passionate about, after all although he was married, he desired his teenage cousin, who happened to be the subject matter of some of his work. In of his most famous photographs 1934's Die Puppe (The Doll), a Gelatin silver print was exhibited in Spain's the Museo Reina (see fig. 26). In an article entitled, *Hans Bellmer Artworks & Famous Photographs,* the author states, "In this photograph a breast, part of the stomach, and the buttocks are exposed, while the angle of the head, gazing at the viewer, makes the face uncharacteristically real. In many of his doll photographs her face is a blank mask onto which the viewer can project whatever they feel, but here she has character" (Hans Bellmer Artworks).

Which brings me to the point, if there is violence in someone's passion now depicted in artwork, how are critics and the public viewing this "violence" as "art." If we are passionate about our creative endeavors do we need to be socially responsible and politically correct? According to artists like Bellmer, the answer is probably no. On the other hand, isn't art supposed to encourage dialogue and thought? Under that definition, Bellmer may be ahead of his time as not only do I continue to study and write about him, but he is frequently covered under photography history textbooks as well as women in the arts courses.

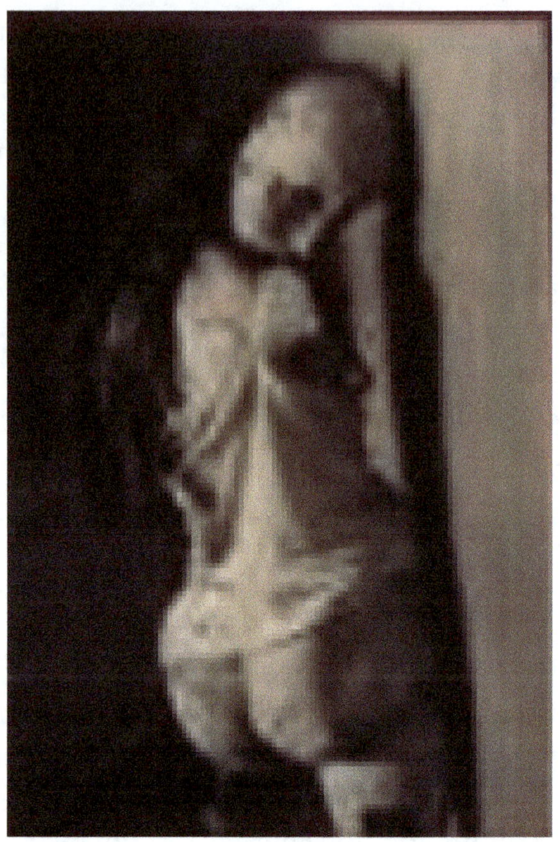

Fig. 26. Hans Bellmer's *Die Puppe (The Doll)*, 1934. This is a gelatin silver print currently exhibited in the Museo Reina Sofia, Spain. www.museoreinasofia.es/en/collection/artwork/die-puppe-doll. Accessed 15 Apr. 2022.

Although Bellmer's messages, in my opinion, may not be very positive nor uplifting, he is exemplifies how one's art can create feelings in others. Additionally, he created what he was passionate about. For instance, what if you lived in the 1970s and loved thrift shopping? This brings me to Cindy Sherman, one of my most inspirational historian and socially reformative photographers.

Cindy Sherman was born in 1954 and constructed identities for over four decades as she mainly works with self portraits. One of the things that fascinated me about Sherman is her love of thrift store shopping and buying props for her shoots. Personally, Sherman is just having a blast while creating her prolific artwork. Not only does she get to get dressed up, select props to create scenes communicates a message, but her photographs have changed how the public sees the world.

Sherman has transformed herself, showcasing a diversity of human archetypes and stereotypes in her photographs. She often works in a photo series, and themes. For example, in the 1970s she tackled feminism, while in the 1980s she was instrumental on helping society deal with the sexual subcultures. In the biographical section for Sherman in the *MoMA* website, the contributors write:

> She often works in series, improvising on themes such as centerfolds (1981) and society portraits (2008). Untitled #216, from her history portraits (1981), exemplifies her use of theatrical effects to embody different roles and her lack of attempt to hide her efforts: often her wigs are slipping off, her prosthetics are peeling away, and her makeup is poorly blended. She highlights the artificiality of these fabrications, a metaphor for the artificiality of all identity construction. (MoMA)

This is another great artist that is just having fun and playing, all the while making photographic history. When someone's work is changing how the world thinks, but they seem to have fun and not "really working" is a sign of true genius and artistic excellence. In an article in the *Artsy* website they elaborate this point:

> Though her work continually re-examines women's roles in history and contemporary society, Sherman resists the notion that her photographs have an explicit

> narrative or message, leaving them untitled and largely open to interpretation. 'I didn't think of what Iwas doing as political,' she once said. 'To me it was a way to make the best out of what I liked to do privately, which was to dress up'. (Artsy)

One of her images, that made me fall in love with her work is called *Untitled Film Still #3*. Cindy Sherman's *Untitled Film Stills* photo series were created in the 1970s and included a total of seventy black and white images (see fig. 27). In these photographs, Sherman posed in a variety of costumes. She often used props to send messages, like the Joy bottle of dis detergent.

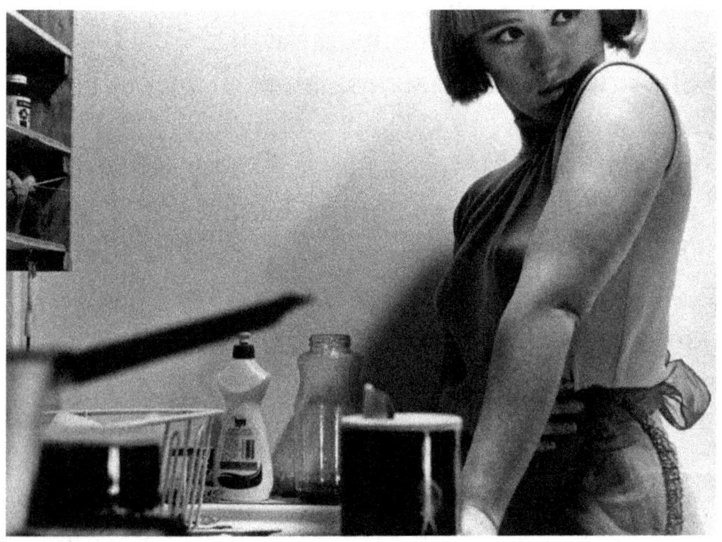

Fig. 27. Cindy Sherman's *Untitled Film Still #3,* 1977, www.moma.org/artists/5392. Accessed 2 April 2022.

Among her characters were a lonely housewife, working girl, and a vamp. The *MoMa* website explains this further:

> Staged to resemble scenes from 1950s and '60s Hollywood, film noir, B movies, and European art-house films, the printed images mimic in format, scale,

> and quality the often-staged "stills" used to promote films. By photographing herself in such roles, Sherman inserts herself into a dialogue about stereotypical portrayals of women. (MoMA)

Another female inspirational artist of mine seems to also follow her passions is Georgia O'Keefe. During her long life from 1887 until 1986 she painted her signature large flowers, New York skyscrapers and amazing New Mexico landscapes. She is considered one of America's most successful and important artists. In the website, *National Museum of Women in the Arts*, the website contributors talk about her development:

> O'Keeffe was strongly influenced by the ideas of Arthur Wesley Dow, who advocated simplifying forms as a means of capturing their essence and developing a personal style. In 1915, following her time with Dow, O'Keeffe destroyed all of her previous work. She returned to the basics, creating radical charcoal drawings that led directly to experiments with total abstraction. (NMWA)

As I often write about Georgia O'Keeffe since I find her so inspirational, I have a calming feeling about her life and fierce determination. It seems that she continued to paint as her life unfolded. She had some difficult situations, like contending with her husband, Alfred Stieglitz's affair. Interestingly, Stieglitz showed O'Keeffe's work for the first time in his gallery. He also was obsessed about photographing O'Keeffe, often using her as his model for his photographic work. She also battled depression episodes. Nevertheless, she continued to flourish as an artist and seemed to paint exclusively where she was at and until the end of her life. For instance, while in Taos, New Mexico her paintings depicted desert landscapes and skulls. "The dry, bright open spaces appealed to her immensely. She continued to paint there until her death at 98. Towards the end of her life, she painted with the help of an assistant due to increasing vision loss" (NMWA).

Not only is her career immensely inspirational to me, but the fact that she continued to paint until the very end, makes me feel serene and happy for her. It also makes me feel like maybe I can continue to create as I get older. In a way, creativity does keep your mind sharp and your intellect utilized. In and article titled, *Aging: What's Art Got To Do With It?*, author Barbara Bagan writes, " Therapeutic art experiences can supply meaning and purpose to the lives of older adults in supportive, nonthreatening ways" (Bagan). Moreover, there is real science backing this up:

> Neurological research shows that making art can improve cognitive functions by producing both new neural pathways and thicker, stronger dendrites. Thus, art enhances cognitive reserve, helping the brain actively compensate for pathology by using more efficient brain networks or alternative brain strategies. Making art or even viewing art causes the brain to continue to reshape, adapt, and restructure, thus expanding the potential to increase brain reserve capacity. (Bagan)

Creating art until the end of your years, seems to be common place for many famous artists. After all, they made a life out of it. Which brings me to my ultimate favorite artists that inspires me to no end since I was eighteen years old. Claude Monet has had a special place in my heart as one of his Japanese bridge waterlilies reproduction was my first art piece I ever purchased. Like Monet, I have always been very passionate about waterlilies and the color combination that he chose. Because of this I lived in waterlilies and his artwork. I had Monet waterlily themed dishes, towels, lamps, bedding, curtains, etc.

Oscar-Claude Monet was a French painter and founder of the impressionist painting movement. He lived from 1840-1926. During his very long career, he loved to paint plein air (in the outdoors). Interestingly, the terminology "Impressionism" comes from the title of one of his paintings called *Impression, soleil levant.* In 1874, it was exhibited in the exhibition of rejects started by Monet and fellow artists as an alternative to the prestigious Salon.

His home in Giverny is the epitome of following your passions (see fig. 28). Monet's paintings were inspired by the lily pond that he had made and created with the help of a gardening crew. What is fascinating to me is that he loved flowers and beautiful landscapes, and made a garden that he tended with love and care for the remaining of his years. Not only that, but then it was this garden that inspired him to paint his masterpieces in all sorts of light. As Monet had said, the light is what of upmost importance.

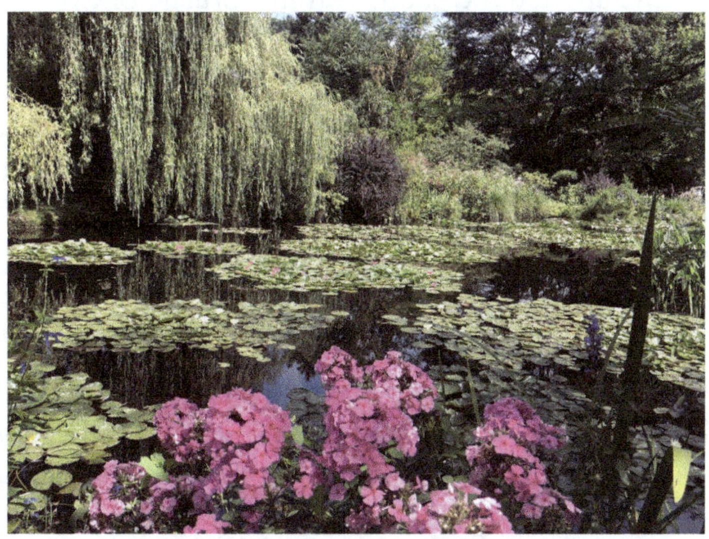

Fig. 28. One of my award winning images taken at Claude Monet's home in Giverny. Claudia Gray. *Monet's Giverny*. 2018, collection of the artist.

Scarlett Thompson, in an article entitled, *Claude Monet and his Water Lilies at the Musée de l'Orangerie,* writes, "He had a passion for flowers, selecting different hybrids of water lilies in an effort to get as many different coloured flowers as possible, deliberately creating his garden as a motif for his paintings" (Thompson, para. 1). I was very fortunate to spend time in Givery at his home and studio and see for myself, and stand where he stood painting. His home and garden were utterly breathtaking. This location inspired me to take photographs of the place and paint my own versions of my waterlilies.

Although Monet painted so many waterlilies, each painting seemed different as he painted them in various color palettes evoking different moods. "In the evening, for example, blues are darker and deeper, evoking a feeling of mystery or reflection. Water lilies have also been painted during sunset hours, providing the canvas with brilliant oranges and yellows creating a sense of warmth and passion" (Thompson, para. 2). His paintings were also so masterful with how he applied the paint with fast brushwork:

> The paint in these paintings has been applied very loosely creating a sense of natural movement. Light is a key subject within these images. Monet has created the illusion of speckles of light in the waters; his lily paintings are some of his most popular and well-known, being synonymous with both the artists' name and the term 'Impressionism' generally. (Thompson, para. 2)

Monet's work is collected around the world at many prestigious galleries and museums. The Musée de l'Orangerie is based in Paris, France. "It holds a significant number of Impressionist and Post - Impressionist paintings, including a gorgeously rich selection of Monet's water lily artwork" (Thompson).

I have been fortunate to see have seen many of his work in person at a variety of venues, after all he is my favorite artist of all time, so I followed his work as much as I could. But a cherished memory of mine that I viewed his work was at the Musée de l'Orangerie. I had heard it was incredible, but I had no idea what to expect.

This museum has the largest pieces of Claude Monet's work. There are eight panels, each measuring two meters high and are 91 meters long. The panels are in two oval rooms forming the infinity symbol. Monet asked for skylights so viewers could see the paintings in natural light. When I was when I entered the rooms, I was not prepared to feel what happened to me. I literally started crying in awe and amazement of someone creating such works of beauty, not only in size, but in a dance of color and harmony (see fig. 29).

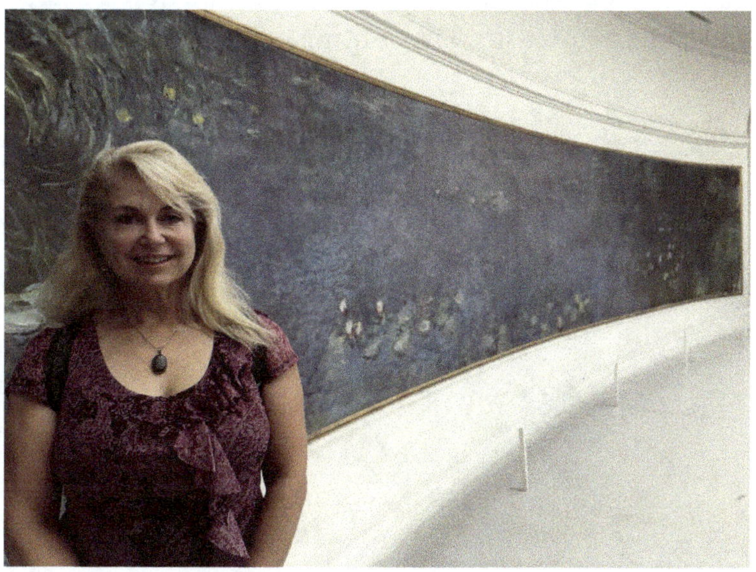

Fig. 29. My Musée de l'Orangerie visit. Alexandra Gray. *Monet's Genuis: Musée de l'Orangerie*. 2019, collection of the artist.

After this museum visit, I started painting my own waterlilies. I didn't want to copy Monet's work, after all he is a master. I mean no one would come close even if they tried. However, I was deeply inspired by his work, colors and I have always felt a sense of calmness around all the various objects that I owned in the waterlilies motif. Some of my paintings were shown at four galleries so far and I have even sold some of them. Somehow, maybe my paintings will never really be as good as this world renowned master, but perhaps my clients can feel the love and calmness I am feeling as I paint my paintings. And from his passion, to my passion, I am creating and perhaps inspiring someone else to have passion, just like he did.

This is just the case that happened with one of my waterlilies paintings. The gallery director was inspired to use my artwork as the promotional piece for marketing material (see fig. 30). And the collector happened to be inspired to purchase the piece (see fig. 31). Because of the quick sale, I was inspired to paint a similar painting. The second painting

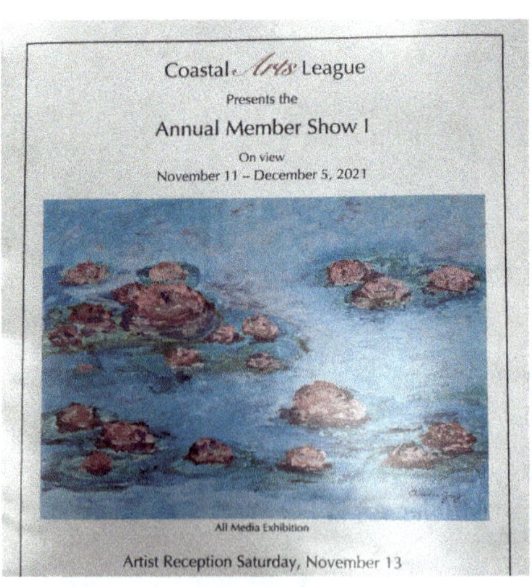


Fig. 30. My waterlilies painting was selected for promotion. Claudia Gray. *Marketing Brochure*. 2021, collection of artist.

in the series hung at the original gallery, and then it was exhibited in another gallery in Santa Cruz (see fig. 32).

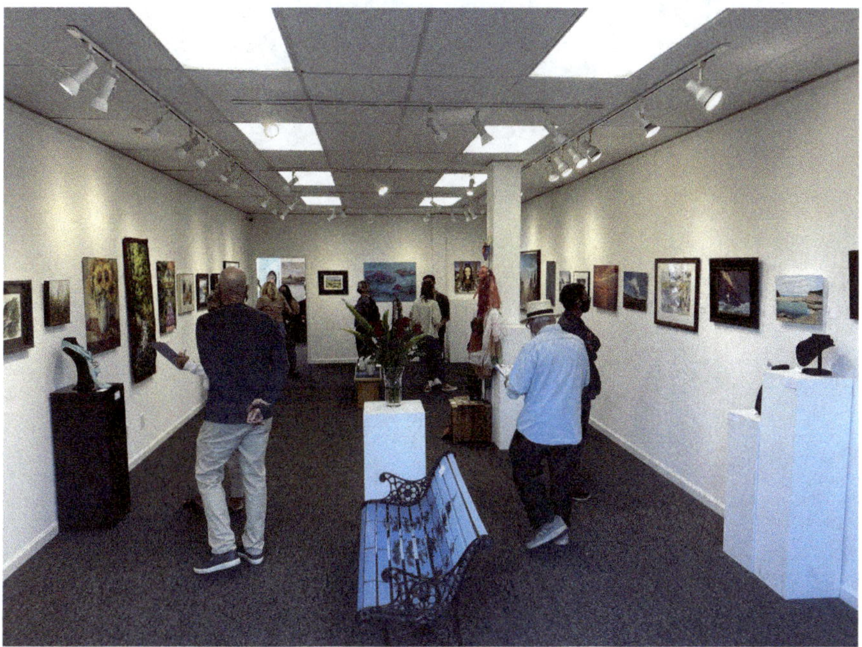

Fig. 31. My painting (back wall) sold at this art show. Claudia Gray. *Gallery Members Show*. 2021, collection of the artist.

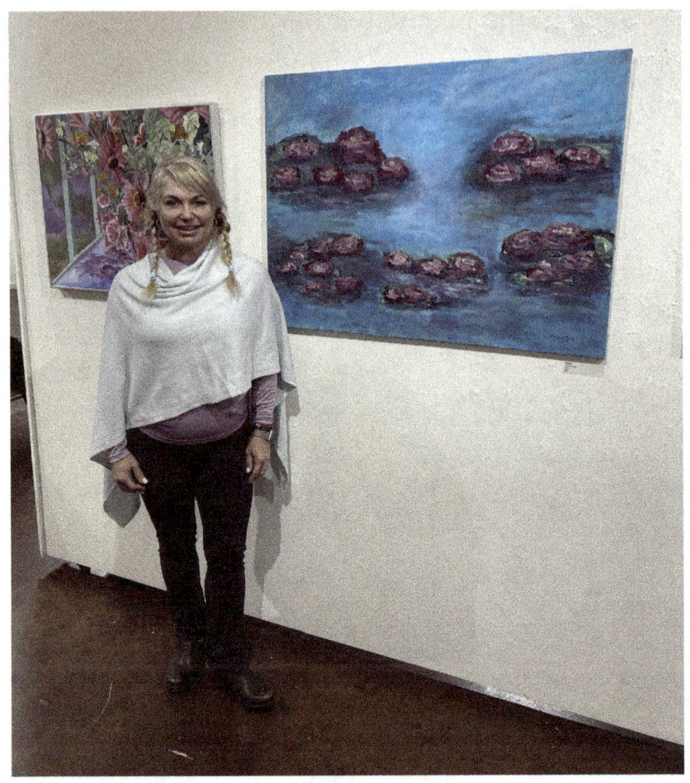

Fig. 32. My second painting in the series, exhibited first at the Half Moon gallery and then most recently at the Santa Cruz Art League Gallery, in Santa Cruz, CA. Claudia Gray. *Repose On Exhibition*. 2022, collection of the artist.

# CHAPTER 7: PHOTOGRAPHY - CAPTURING MOMENTS IN TIME

One thing I realized that no matter what, especially with the smart phone camera, is that I can create photographic art any time I want and where ever I am. Photography has been a long time passion of mine. It originally started in high school when I worked for a modeling agency and would see many of the models look sporty and cute with their big sweatshirts as they came to the agency. At a later date, I would then see their proofs from their modeling shoot and thought wow, who is this ultra sexy vixen? Is that really that girl next door that came into the reception area the other week?

I was also in the modeling pool and my portfolio showed such pictures as well, although I was a constant tom-boy, beach person who lived in sports attire (I still do). But in any event, even though modeling was not my thing, what I did learn with this early experience in my life, is that you can portray something in photographs that may or may not originally be there. You can always also capture a moment in time, freeze time, and tell a story from it.

As I became a freelance writer in the late 1990s, I was in need of photographs to support my stories. This is when my photography took on a new life, and it developed into photojournalism. My images were being published along with my stories, so they needed to be professional quality. In my mind, I went back to those times, when I would take pictures both behind the camera as a model trying to remember what made a good shot. Make sure to get the white of the eyes. Get that facial expression that correlates with the story. Make sure to fill 80% of the frame. And, try to evoke emotion from an image. This served me well and it continued to take a huge role in my life.

At this point in my life, I started to have kids. And I was thrilled to realize that my babies were a newfound gold mind of photographic subject matter! Most moms love taking pictures of their babies and I was no different. So for a couple of decades, I continued to take pictures of the family in all sorts of different ways. Yes, I was probably that person that took too many pictures at a birthday party, but I have a well documented family history. All joking aside, when the kids were a little older, I started to really notice good landscape photography. I especially paid close attention to professional nature photographers. With TV on demand in full swing by now, I started to watch all of Art Wolfe's TV shows on how to take nature and wildlife photographs. Somewhere along the line, I was fascinated with photographers like Peter Lik, and of course, my ultimate inspiration, Ansel Adams.

It was around the time that I started to exhibit and I already had my first art show under my belt. Because I loved the great outdoors and would often photograph it, I concluded

I had enough images to frame and start selling them. As a result that I have always had a love of nature, true pure joy, and love for it, I like to believe that my passion comes through in my photographs. I remember saying that my mission as a photographer was to bring nature to people that may not be able to get to places that I was photographing. Many of the places I would take photographs, such as in Yosemite, were places that I would backpack to or arrive after a very strenuous hike. So I understood that your average viewer may not be able to do that in order to see that vista.

My best selling, "Double Vernal Rainbow" was one of those days where I went at the time the rainbow was to hit the waterfall, and then by me moving around I was able to capture two rainbows (see fig. 33). People like Ansel Adams taught me that you work with Mother Nature in order to freeze that special gift she is letting you witness. For me, one of the best part of this gift is being able to share it with others.

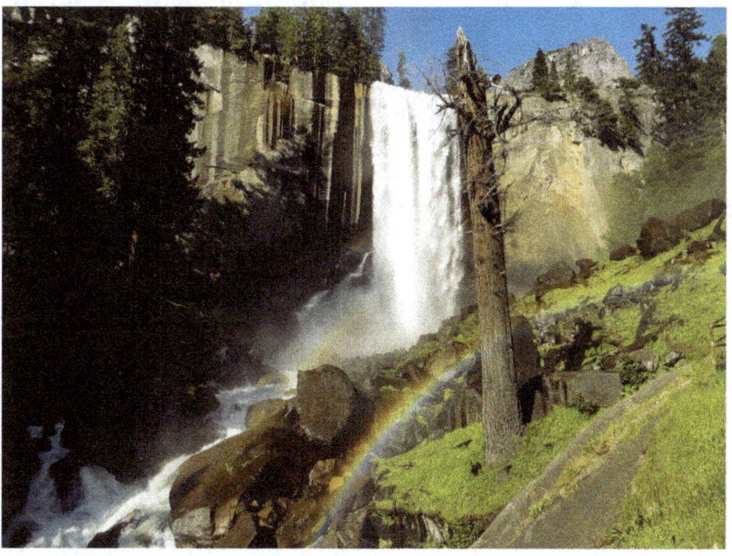

Fig. 33. Claudia Gray. *Vernal Double Rainbow*. 2017, collection of the artist.

It was during my studies for my masters program that I formally studied artists that have been very inspirational to me for years. These were art history giants, such as, Cindy Sherman and Ansel Adams to name a few. As I wrote about their lives and how they created, I learned that there were a few similarities we shared. Perhaps these are even attributes of the majority of creative people possess. For instance, some artists are lucky to figure out how to live out their lives in a creative flow. In reading about Ansel Adams, I would say he was definitely one of these fortunate folks.

I found that studying about Ansel Adams was also like learning about what I liked and felt inspired by. For instance, we were both completely in love with Yosemite National Park. Adams is well loved and known for his technical black and white images he took in Yosemite. At the early age of fourteen years old in 1916, he was given a Kodak Box Brownie camera for his birthday present. It was around that time that he started taking his first photographs of Yosemite National Park while on a family vacation. It is a full circle situation as these photographs were taken at the same spots that many years later he would return to create iconic images that propelled him into photography history books. Ansel Adams recounts the his life-long creativity from the start of his childhood family vacation:

> That first impression of the valley—white water, azaleas, cool fir caverns, tall pines and stolid oaks, cliffs rising to undreamed-of heights, the poignant sounds and smells of the Sierra…was a culmination of experience so intense as to be almost painful. From that day in 1916 my life has been colored and modulated by the great earth gesture of the Sierra. (qtd. in Turnage, para. 7)

Interestingly, the decision to become a professional photographer was not clear, as he found himself with a fork in the road. Around 1927, as a twenty-five year-old, he ended up choosing a life in the arts over a musical career as a concert pianist. Some say, he selected not photography, but choose Yosemite over music. He wrote this to his future wife, Virginia Best, "Music is wonderful – but the musical world is the *bunk*! So much petty doing - so much pose an insincerity and distorted values.... It seems very clear to me now that unless I get more of the outdoors, I will blow up. I find myself looking back on the golden days and Yosemite with supreme envy" (Adams 13).

Somehow I understood what Adams was experiencing as when creativity gets a hold of you there's a lot of passion and inspiration that shows up. It sometimes feels like there's outside forces at work. Some call these muses and if they exist, which I believe they exist for me, and Adams' muses kept calling him to Yosemite National Park. In a way, like they have welcomed me there many times throughout my life. Adams commented to Virginia on what he was feeling, "I think I came closer to really living then than at any other time in my life, because I was closer to elemental things - was not so introspective, so damn sensitive, so infernally discriminative" (Adams 13). In my mind, and most of the photography world, there is no doubt Ansel Adams selected the right life journey.

Overall, I believe that Ansel Adams used his talents and life for good causes. Other major environmental groups agreed as he was recognized in various ways. For instance, the Sierra Club made the Ansel Adams Award for Conservation Photography in 1971. The Wilderness Society established the Ansel Adams Award for Conservation in 1981. This environmental organization has some of his photographs on exhibition at a permanent and large gallery in Washington, D.C., at their headquarters. One of his greatest awards was receiving the Presidential Medal of Freedom from Jimmy Carter in 1980 for his contributions to the National Park Service. The citation reads:

> At one with the power of the American landscape, and renowned for the patient scale in timeless beauty of his work, photographer Ansel Adams has been visionary in his efforts to preserve the countries wild and scenic areas, both on film and on earth. Drawn to the beauty of natures monuments, he is regarded by environmentalist as a monument himself, and by photographers as a national institution. It is through his foresight and fortitude that so much of America has been saved for future Americans. (Adams and Alinder 295)

In 2017, I was fortunate enough to be selected to volunteer for Yosemite from a pool of four hundred applicants as the hiring Park Ranger revealed to me. She said it really helped that I was already a certified Wilderness First Responder, but they loved that I had been photographing Yosemite for the last twenty plus years. I was delighted and I could not pass up this life long dream of working in some capacity for the National Park Service. Yes, my pay would be zero, but I knew the payment in form of overall experiences and adventure I would receiving could not be measured in a monetary sense. I felt like my compensation would be priceless.

During my six weeks there, before and after my work shifts, I would have free time to explore the park and take photographs. These were very special times for me as I made friends with the Rangers, park employees and even a Bear Specialist. The Bear Specialist was also a budding photographer and we went on many photo shoots including trying to capture the elusive moonbow, which we did on two separate evenings. These lunar rainbows are rare occurring about less than ten percent as normal rainbows. These require additional conditions to form, and you need to be standing just in the right spot. Interestingly, it was on this trip that I learned about this optical phenomenon that is caused by the moon's light refracted through water droplets in the air.

With my newfound park friends, as we hung out, we often chatted about the happenings of the park and what was worth photographing that day. Sometimes, I would just wonder around on my own trying to see what would catch my eye. I remember often jumping on my bike because there was a bear siting. Although, I captured many of these photographs of the wondrous black bear, there is a special photograph that I will always hold in my heart as the embodiment of connection with nature and completely being in the zone.

During the hundreds of photographs that I took of these wondrous dragonfly creatures, as there happened to be a few of them cooperating with me, I felt an extreme sense of gratefulness and calmness. It might have helped that I was very slow in my movement and I stayed in the same spot for many minutes at a time. It might have helped that I did not make any unnecessary noise or fast movements. I sat there and watched, I became part of the environment, and they accepted me. I remember holding my breath as I would snap the shots (see fig. 34). I remember moving my hands very slowly and methodically. They didn't seem to mind that I was there, I perhaps was part of the bushes that they were exploring. Either way, I felt privileged and a sense of connection to be taking such images with these very flighty insects. At the very end of the photo shoot, I remember exhaling very deeply and thinking wow that was really intense and I loved it! I was definitely in an alternate state of consciousness.

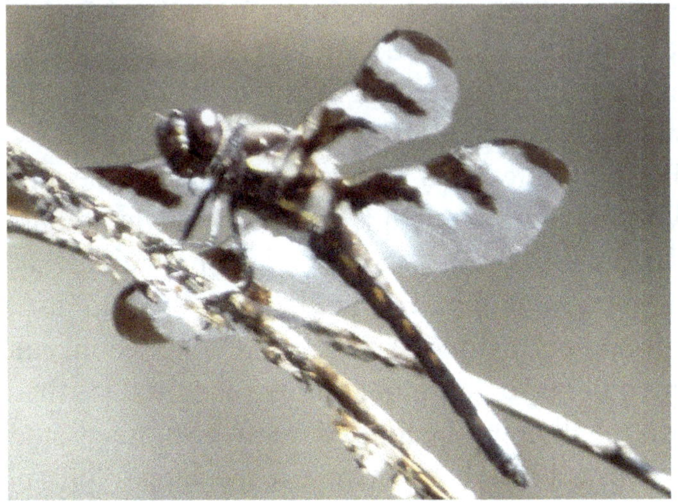

Fig. 34. Claudia Gray. *Dragonfly Breaths*. 2017, collection of the artist.

Some people call this zone phase "flow." This is where time stands still and there is almost a spiritual experience in the silence of creating and connection. Susan Sontag, a well respected novelist and modernism critic wrote many pieces on silence as a component in aesthetic. In "The Aesthetics of Silence," an essay from her 1969 collection entitled, *Styles of Radical Will*, she explores how silence mediates the role of art as a form of spirituality in a secular world:

> Though no longer a confession, art is more than ever a deliverance, an exercise in asceticism. Through it, the artist becomes purified — of himself and, eventually, of his art, The artist (if not art itself) is still engaged in a progress toward 'the good.' But formerly, the artist's good was mastery of and fulfillment in his art. Now

> it's suggested that the highest good for the artist is to reach that point where those goals of excellence become insignificant to him, emotionally and ethically, and he is more satisfied by being silent than by finding a voice in art. (Sontag, para. 2)

There's another great quote that I love. Bruce Garrabrandt eloquently states, "Creativity doesn't wait for that perfect moment. It fashions its own perfect moments out of ordinary ones" (Johnson). I love this quote, because creativity is everywhere in the world. Simple and ordinary things that is no big deal to Mother Nature are BIG deals to us humans. Take the lighting up of Horsetail Falls for example. I have been lucky enough to be there at the right time which only happens once a year for approximately three weeks. Moreover, the conditions have to be just right, for instance, no snow, or rain, etc. I have been lucky enough to have taken this technical shot three different years (see fig. 35).

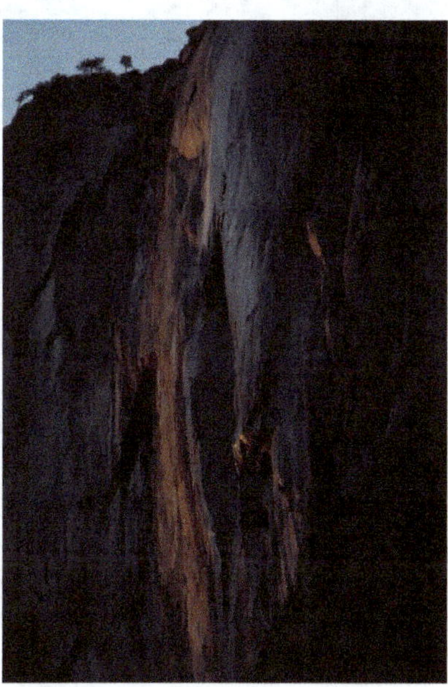

Fig. 35. My award winning Horsetail Falls image taken the first year I attempted the shot. Claudia Gray. *Horsetrail Falls.* 2013, collection of the artist.

At first I thought, hey what's the big deal, but as I talked to fellow photographers in the crowds, sometimes I heard this would have been their X number of years without luck. The largest number I heard was held by a Midwest photographer that attempted it eight different years. Wow, I thought, maybe he wasn't nice to Mother Nature or somehow didn't have good nature karma, I don't know... However, what that taught me was to take each moment and carpe diem - for that matter carpe each second because if you have ever been to this event, the show only lasts literally about ten minutes each day for you to get a good shot (see fig. 36).

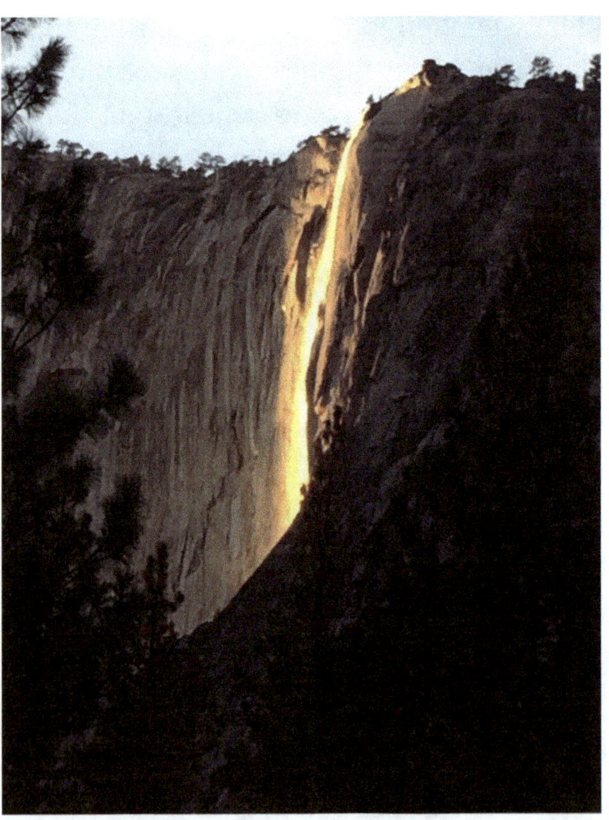

Fig. 36. Another year and angle at Horsetail Falls, Yosemite. Claudia Gray. *Horsetrail Falls Glow.* 2016, collection of the artist.

In photography, a minute can be a lifetime and you might miss the shot if you hesitate. Personally, I believe that all my years of practice with meditation and studying Eastern Philosophy, specifically Buddhism, I have come to the understanding that one must have mindfulness when trying to get a good shot. If you are not in the present moment, you might lose the shot. There are even photography courses for mindfulness. In the *Udemy* website the description for their course offering states:

> Mindful Photography provides you with the opportunity to use what you see as your anchor; in much the same way as when you meditate you use your breath as an anchor.When you are out creating photographs, the visual experience becomes your primary sensory concern. (Udemy)

This type of mindfulness photography can happen anywhere and once you start doing it, it is very meditative and relaxing. The *Udemy* website explains:

> You can be sitting or walking, observing your surroundings. Every time you notice that your mind has wandered off - planning a shot, dreaming of a photographic possibility, worrying about your ability or even just thinking about later in the day - you come back to the visual experience. (Udemy)

I experience this type meditative state very often when I am doing my underwater photography. I love swimming in between the yellow tangs and sea turtles (not touching them or getting too close, as this is prohibited by Hawaiian law). The trick I have found is to just blend. Again, like with the insects, I am super slow with my movements and I might be shooting for an hour in the same spot. Be forewarned that this may be super annoying to your travel companions.

This is the case I have experienced time and time again where my travel buddies are not as photographically obsessed or perhaps are not really meditating like I am while swimming. And so, after about twenty or thirty minutes they are back to shore. Yet, for me the water is very soothing and I lose track of time because I am in the zone, meditating and in my happy place. Why would I want to leave this glorious scene? Nevertheless, my body also has needs so I know when to take a break. Knowing in my core that safety is paramount in the water or in the great outdoors, I listen to my body. So I usually stay out until I am a little tired, hungry or chilly, which is a couple of hours for me.

One of the secrets to photography I have learned is for the wildlife not to notice you, or perhaps have them accept you as part of the surroundings. The way to accomplish this is to be as still as possible (see fig. 37). I know you say, but I am underwater how do I do that? Well, practice and try to move slowly and try not to make any noise if possible. I know…

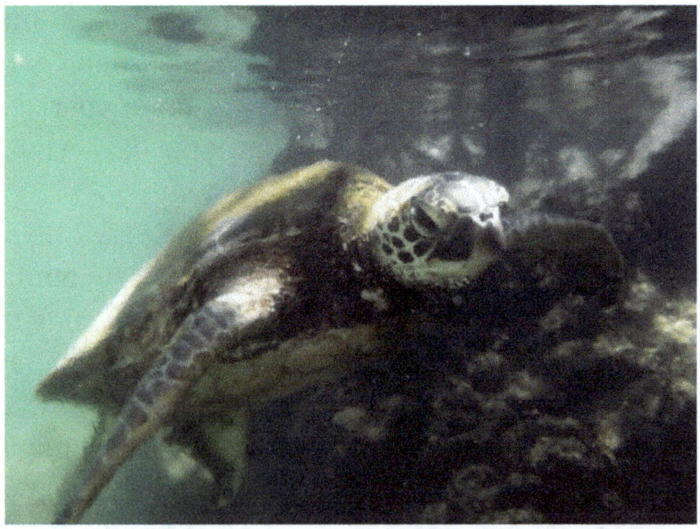

Fig. 37. One of my favorite underwater subjects to photograph, the Hawaiian green sea turtle. Claudia Gray. *Honu.* 2015, collection of the artist.

you are probably saying, but I want to talk to my friend about the cool sea life that just swam by. Well, you can't, at least not yet, wait until you get back to shore. But don't fret, as there's a way to communicate. For instance, I have developed and often use hand signals to interact with my companions. The nice thing about blending into the surroundings, is the wildlife don't get spooked. Hence, you can get their eyes, and not get the beginner photographer fish back shots, where all you are getting is the backside of the fish as they swim away from you (see fig. 38).

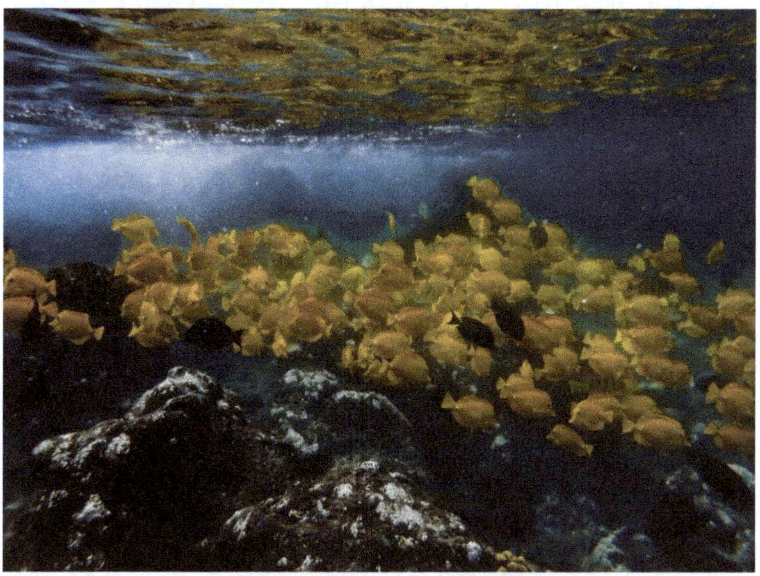

Fig. 38. A school of Yellow Tangs with the sun shining through the water, causing a colorful reflection of the fish toward the top of the ocean. Claudia Gray. *Zambrosas*. 2019, collection of the artist.

Two other secrets to photography are what I believe to be pretty obvious. They are, like real estate, location, location, location. And like the stock market, timing is key, selling and buying stocks just at the right time are crucial to making profits. Well, photography is just like that. If you want to take a picture of the Milky Way, you cannot do that during the day, and you cannot do it in a lighted city locale. Yes, you will have to stay up late, most likely, and research when and where the Milky Way will be appearing. Additionally, you will have to find a place where it will be visible and not diminished with city lights. Sure, there are other components to taking a good shot like this, for example getting the technical settings to your camera and understanding night time photography. But all these things are possible with some research and practice.

Photography doesn't believe in punching a clock. For instance, for my Milky Way shot that won a cash award, I hiked up to Glacier Point by myself and took the shot around midnight or an hour later (see fig. 39). I was alone and I

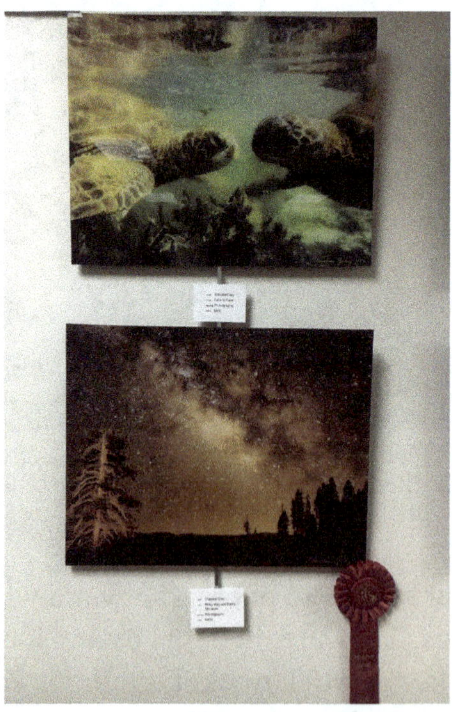

Fig. 39. Two of my photographs at the Los Gatos Art Association Juried Art Show held at the JCC's Gallery. Claudia Gray. *Juried Photographs*. 2017, collection of the artist.

planned out my trip. I was also in frequent phone contact with a Ranger friend, so he knew my location. Of course, there has to be some luck component and cooperation from Mother Nature. If the sky was all cloudy or raining, it would not have worked. I did the same thing when I climbed Sentinel Dome on my own to get another shot of the Milky Way on another evening. These were my perks to living and volunteering in Yosemite for my six weeks. Remember my compensation: adventure and experiences equal priceless. So during this time, I could afford to go back again to the right location and time. What I am trying to explain, is that if you really want to take a shot of something in Nature or anywhere in the world, you have to commit to doing it. Get yourself out there, plan it, research it, and try it. If you don't you might not capture that moment in time you got to witness.

You might think oh it will happen again, but sometimes it just does not. Case and point, in my photograph "Pele Awakes" (Gray) on a trip to see the Hawai'i Volcanoes National Park with my family, I specifically wanted to take some lava shots. Back in the early nineties I lived in Hawaii so I was fascinated and connected to anything Hawaiian. I had a deep respect for Pele and I wanted to showcase her in my photography.

On this shot, I had planned it out and I needed to be at the park at this location by four in the morning Hawaiian time, which means it's a couple hours earlier there than in California. This was a huge commitment, body wise, but it was well worth it. During the pre-sunrise time, the sky lit up a beautiful color and crater was glowing magnificently. I ended up using my best tool, my feet. So somehow I decided that the tree in front of the crater would be a cool shot. And luckily, once again Mother Nature and Pele cooperated (see fig. 40). This picture has also been one of my best sellers and has been exhibited at numerous shows and galleries.

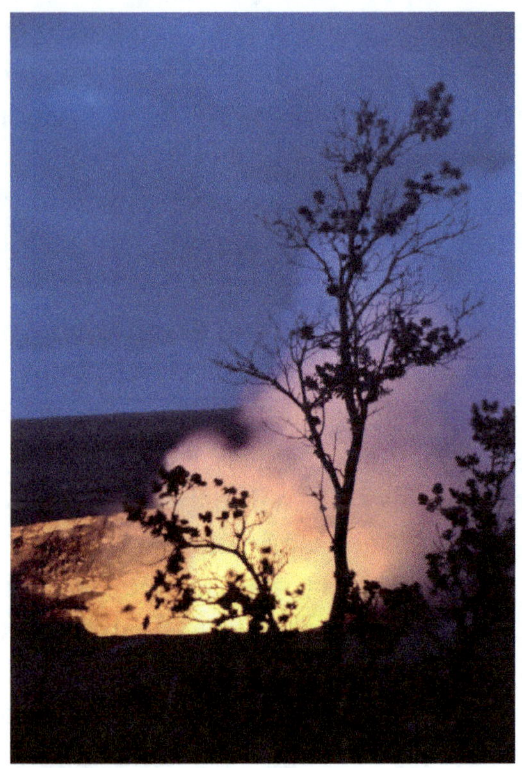

Fig. 40. Claudia Gray. *Pele Awakes*. 2015, collection of the artist.

Going back to what I what I was alluding to earlier, that sometimes you don't get a second shot to photograph something. It's not just your life and circumstances, it has to do more with the location and the things are constantly in flux in the world. A couple of years later the same crater can looked vastly different. I also once heard that the tree I took a picture of is no longer there due to current lava flow. But more importantly, craters and locations get reshaped by Pele all the time. The National Park Service writes:

> With less magma left to support the summit, Halema‘uma‘u crater began to collapse. Every 28 hours on average, the ground within the summit caldera of Kīlauea sank with dramatic collapse events. By the end of the 2018 eruption, Halema‘uma‘u crater had sunk by 1,600 feet (488m), and its diameter more than doubled. (National Park Service)

And of course, Pele is probably not done with her plans, so whatever shot you take now may be a historical snippet in time as well.

# CHAPTER 8: DEFINING AND ACCEPTING MY OWN CREATIVITY PHILOSOPHY

It is interesting how life works. The past two years have been the hardest in my whole life. Sure, there's been ups and downs, but nothing like the pervasive waves of negativity and loss. I am reminded of an old saying, and in the universe I believe in, is that it does not give you more than you can handle. Insert God or whatever religion flavor choice, but you will not have more than you can handle. This mantra kept me going as I chuckled to myself, I thought, wow, I must be able to handle quite a bit!

After all, it is not every year that all at once there are massive life changes. In the last two years, I endured a divorce, having an empty nest, learning to live on my own in a new place, moving contents of the family house due to the sale, selling my beloved chicken flock, lost the use of my studio and kilns, healing from several pesky medical conditions born out from the chronic stress of all the situations commingling in such a short period of time. All of this, plus the global pandemic of COVID-19 which compromised many activities, travel, induced fear and created more uncertainty. Just when I thought things couldn't get worse, I lost my beloved fourteen and a half year-old cocker spaniel, Max, who developed a fatal renal condition and passed away in January 2022. I watched, nurtured and nursed my best friend to the end. I thought that has to be the icing on the cake of loss, and that must be the turning point.

Through my grief cycle of seeing how the family was going to function and the dynamics behind it, learning how to be an independent women, and keeping my health in check, I was often reminded of the beautiful water lilies that grow in muck. I often thought how lucky and a bit crazy I was to continue to work on my Masters through this time. I sometimes felt overwhelmed, but at other times I felt blessed to have something ground me and occupy my brain with positive information.

I found that I loved writing again and it was a welcomed part of my day to develop school discussion posts or papers. The universe had gifted me enough to keep me from being swallowed up from the loss. My creativity helped me through the immense loss years. It wasn't all dark and gloomy. Being an extrovert and having much support, I knew that I needed to keep the brain functioning with fun. After all, I was a product from the 80's "work hard, play hard" mentality. So at times, I played hard and let off some steam.

During this time I was enrolled in a Creative and Its Development masters class while juggling all of my life's curve balls. Albeit, at times it was impossible for me to focus or carve out enough time to complete the assignments. However, I found it like therapy because it was hugely instrumental in reminding me of who I was and AM. Through my time in exploring creativity, learned that I AM a creative being. Not just because I like to make things, but it was here through my formal studies is where I learned and took to heart all the ideals and philosophies that help define and expand one's creativity.

I remember the tortured feelings of longing to create in my studio under the majestic redwood trees where for approximately eight years I felt safe and free to create. I remember listening to hours and hours of monks chanting in the background as I infused these positive vibes into the glass artwork I was making. I remember losing time as I flowed in a beautiful zone, and what I thought were minutes turned into hours. I literally would lose time, or did I gain time as I was enthralled in my work? I realized that was very satisfying to me. Not only did that make me happy, but also amazingly serene.

And now, how I lamented the fact that now days, I could no longer fill the kilns with glass art. I remember the firing days were so much fun because the next day, I would return and open the kiln's lid to see how the firing processed. I always said it felt like Christmas morning because you didn't know what you were going to get. Those moments were full of anticipation as I witnessed what fired correctly and how the pieces turned out (or didn't turn out).

In Rollo May's book, *The Courage To Create,* he writes about the ideals of creativity as related to the unconscious, encounters, and creating oneself. I found this theory fascinating and I resonated with what he was saying. May discusses anxiety and writes, "…that anxiety comes from *not being able to know the world you're in, not being able to orient yourself in your own existence*" (May 58). May asserts creative folks have much anxiety, stating, "…even though a high price may be paid in terms of insecurity, sensitivity, and defensiveness for the gift of the divine madness, to borrow the term used by the classic cut Greeks" (May 93). He expounds this point further by writing, "They do not run away from non-being, but by encountering and wrestling with it, force it to produce being. They knock on silence for an answering music; they pursue meaninglessness until they can force it to mean" (May 93).

As I kept my head above the water of grief, I was grateful and grounded by the water lilies of my creativity. I realized that not only would my creativity not die, but I would help it flower again - even in the icky muck. As I continued reading different philosophers, art history, various artists, and writings, I started began to see that I was forming my own creative theory. I am sure if I put some thought to it, I would have created one in the past, however, having my own theory was new to me, as I just made stuff and why would I think about having a theory anyway, it didn't make sense. I just wanted to make art. But at this time, my own creative theory emerged, and one that definitely resonated with the intensity of my life that I was experiencing at this time.

I came to the conclusion, at this particular juncture on my life path as an artist, my journey's current bus-stop, was at this personal creative theory. I am sure this ideal may fluctuate or develop as my life circumstances change. However, my current theory can be summed up accordingly: creativity results from emotional expression and self preservation.

The idea did not materialize one day out of the blue, nor did I come up with it on my own. Instead, the ideal grew slowly from a seedling of philosophy in a class reading. Then it continued to develop as I strived to create with what little I had on hand, even though I did not have a studio any more and everything was in storage. The ideal flourished and took a firm form as I decided on starting a new photo series. The project's name would be, "A Woman's Work Is Never Done." Like a water lily in muck, it flowered and took form. The photo series ended up having a life of its own and served me well throughout its creative process.

Consciously, I was definitely feeling a lot of anxiety not knowing how I would be able to create without my studio and tackling the huge tasks of managing all the changes with the divorce, sale of the home, partial empty nest, and trying to figure out how to successfully live on my own. And perhaps, this might be where my personal creative ideals and self preservation thoughts began to be conceived. As I was not creating actively, there was anxiety building up for not being able to produce. I also became aware of how fast time was being felt with each passing week. But these were not the only practical issues I was contending with. Other sources of anxieties included, being completely unorganized due to the move and not having my artistic supplies readily available.

In my classes, I was prompted to discuss creativity and what seemed to come out on the pages was me writing about how I perplexed on how to continue to create without my beloved studio. I was not only grief-stricken, but practically not able to fire glass artwork. Not only did I think about this as I looked at my glass sculptures that may be a timely piece of my creativity, like when an artist dies and can't produce anymore artwork. I reflected if I was alive, but in a way dead?

It was during one of these mornings, after sharing one of my essays on the closing of my studio with my fellow masters students, friends and my older daughter, that I awoke from a very vivid dream. I woke up and realized that the studio does not define me. I define the studio. Moreover, I AM THE STUDIO! So now, I had a sense of renewal and purpose. Even though I do not have my studio, I can still create, but how? Did my muses whisper this realization in my dream? I pondered if I could figure it out and if they may be continuing to help me plan a course on how I was going to proceed.

In actuality, there were definite cravings, needs and yearnings to create. I was anxious to create… but how, and with what time? Somehow, my muses came to help and as my artist self preservation needs won out. I realized I could still create with very few items. So, after much deliberation and planning, I settled on making self portrait photographs like historically socially reformative photographer, Cindy Sherman. Immensely inspired by her work since I first was introduced many years ago, my images would also have a social message and emotional expression component to them.

With this theory in mind of self preservation and self expression, I would initiate my own therapy like May's Greek gods. And by doing so, I would soothe myself with expressing the shear volume of work that I encountered and felt overburdened by. I contemplated the photo series name quite a bit, and ended up choosing, "A Woman's Work Is Never Done." The series provided a balance of fun and personal emotional expression of my overburdened workload, physical exhaustion and tired mind.

Having the validation of being able to create again, through this project, I felt like I was self preserving. Furthermore, I expressed my excruciating emotions in the photographic art images. Photographs from the series, "The Irony of Ironing" (see fig. 41) and "Endless Dust" (see fig. 42) would further express and illustrate my feelings of futility of the massive workload I was undertaking.

There is no doubt, that the various philosopher exposure assisted me to even form my own creative theory. After all, do most artist have one? I know I did not even think

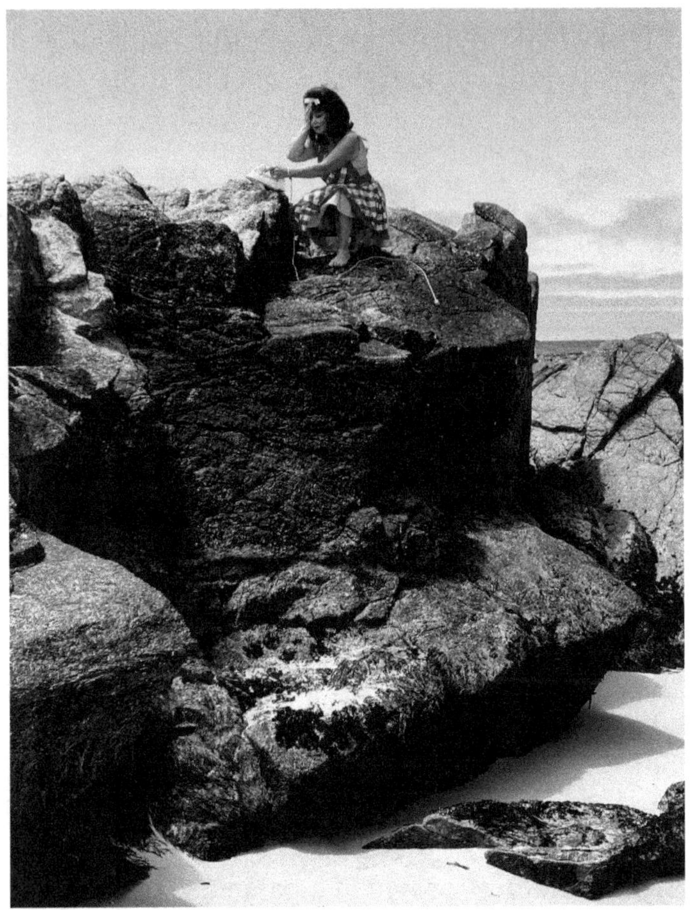

Fig. 41. Claudia Gray. *The Irony of Ironing*. 2021, collection of the artist.

twice about it during the many years that I happily produced work. I just created because it was fun and I was curious. But there is a reason why some are called to create. The answer may lie in one's mind.

Carl Jung discusses polarity explaining how there is a relationship between the consciousness and unconscious minds. Rollo May talked about what Jung believed and said, "The relationship was compensatory; consciousness controls the wild, illogical vagaries of the unconscious, while the

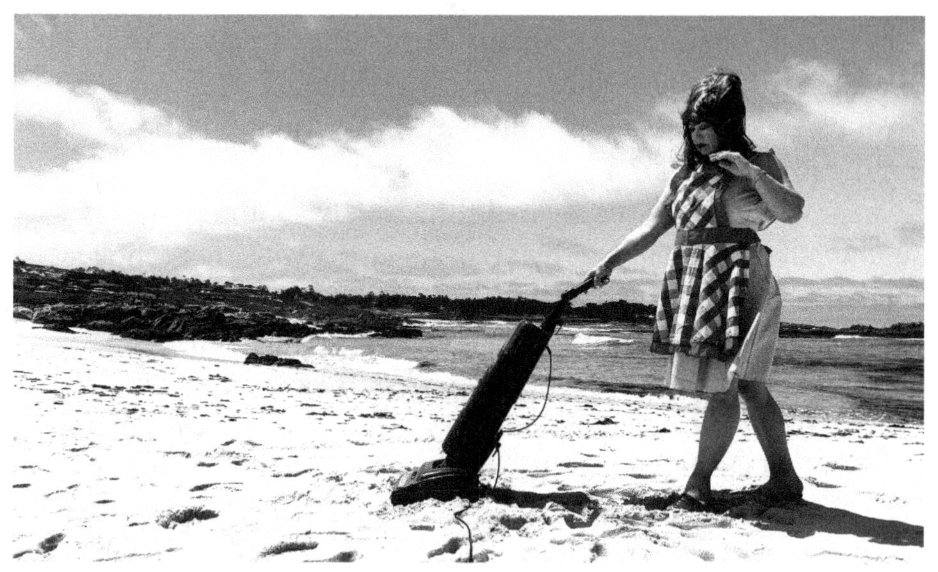

Fig. 42. Claudia Gray. *Endless Dust*. 2021, collection of the artist.

unconscious keeps consciousness from drying up in banal, empty, arid rationality" (May 59). And so I contemplated that how I felt as I was all dressed up at one of my photo shoots for the series, at one of the beaches, dressed in my Stepford wife costume.

At this particular shoot, I was at a Carmel beach doing manual housework. I purposefully reveled in the juxtaposition of the mundane ironing chore assisted by an electric iron at the beach, of course, unplugged. The photography entitled, "The Irony of Ironing" features me on top of a very large wrinkly beach rock attempting to iron it and there's frustration on my face.

The image named, "Endless Dust," shows me happily vacant and vacuuming the beach sand with the water and a beautiful cloud in the background. These photos show a merging of the subconscious and conscious minds, and a commingling of the expression of emotion.

As I continued to develop the series and shot more images, I reflected on May's anxiety statements. I concluded that I can succinctly agree with May. Furthermore, I was putting myself back into the world of artists and creativity. Somehow, I was intuitively and formatively soothing myself and my anxieties that had ben building up. I was both relieved and delighted that instead of feeling like I had more work, the photo series seemed to give my unconscious and conscious minds a fun stage to act itself out and start healing.

Not only did the photo series resurrect my creativity, but it ended up flowering and continues to live. I was surprised and amazed of how many venues it took form. The series first was shown at the main part of the gallery in Half Moon Bay were I was one of the curators of the Mixed Media show. It was also displayed in another part of the gallery where my other items are for sale throughout the year. Two of the pictures were exhibited in the Hayward Public Library Gallery and a San Francisco gallery. The photo series also was my big project for the Creativity and Its Development class. The series was selected to be included at the Tiffin University Student Conference, and it ended up winning an award. Two photographs from the series were accepted and exhibited in a juried photography exhibit at a Santa Cruz gallery which then prompted the gallery manager to schedule with me an upcoming mini-exhibition just for this series. The greeting cards and photographs continue to be consistent sellers, and they have been part of several art clubs and the National Pen Women Association meeting presentations or displays. I was also surprised, that I had multiple sales from the project, as these photos were edgy and not pretty art.

This series definitely had a purpose. As a creative human, I had a yearning to self-preserve, to continue to create, and to go back to my existence as an artist. I had already lost too much and healing needed to take place. Additionally, I did not want to lose my ability to create and put form to an inspiration. This following quote from Rollo May's book really assisted in my comprehension of what I was intuitively doing. It also explained how important my own theory was becoming as I continued to create and tackle each of life's tasks. May states:

> The compensation also works on specific problems: if I consciously been too far one-way on some issue, my unconscious willing the other way. This is, of course, the reason why the more we are unconsciously smitten with our doubts about an idea, the more dogmatically we fight for it in our conscious arguments. (May 59)

I reflected on how I pacified myself being expressive of my subconscious thoughts and even sometimes my real conscious pain. May explained, "The self is made up, and it's growing edge, of the models, farms, metaphors, myths and all other kinds of psychic content which gives it direction and it's self-creation" (May 99). As an artist and creative being, I resonated with how his quote continued to evolve in my mind, "Thinking and self creating are inseparable. When we become aware of all the fantasies in which we see ourselves in the future, pilot ourselves this way or that, this becomes obvious" (May 99).

This ideal is also illustrated in another photograph that I selected for the photo series. The image is called "Delusional Denial" (see fig. 43) It shows a woman with her head tilted back as she is laughing with joy, however there is a man who holds her neck with an ominous look in his eyes as he stares into the camera. Because I used focus groups for this project to get a feel if I was on the right track and so one. I learned from the focus groups that this image created a lot of emotional stirrings. What I could surmise was that this

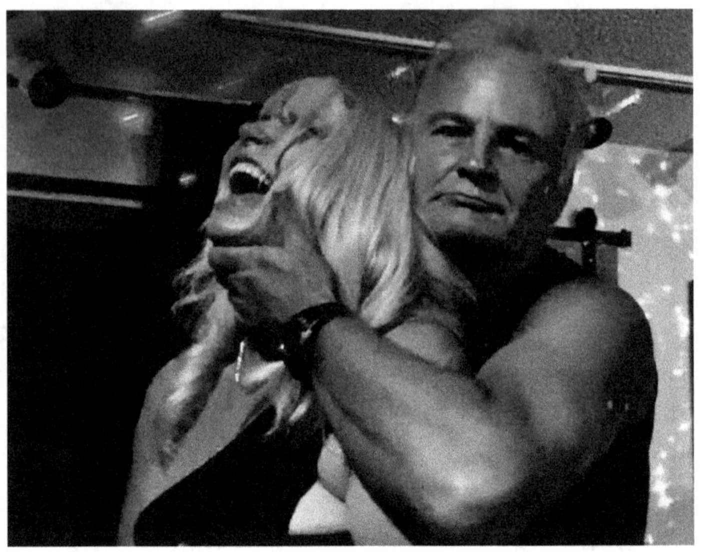

Fig. 43. Claudia Gray. *Delusional Denial.* 2021, collection of the artist.

photograph was powerful as it made most people feel uncomfortable, especially the women I polled. Ultimately, I could commiserate as it made me uneasy as well. However, it was this raw emotional unbalance that the photo produced in the audience that got the attention of the gallery manager offering me a mini-exhibition for this photo series. This photo touched an emotional cord in people.

Subconsciously, I know exactly why I made that image part of the series. I understood that I was playing out what I was experiencing in real life. Part of my unconscious mind was experiencing a curtain of denial from my past and present. The image was a commination of nonacceptance of my life events. Delusion. Denial. The girl in the photograph was delusionally in denial. I also know that how I felt is not in isolation to only my life events, there are many people in denial situations that can relate to the image, characters and content.

I further contemplated that emotional expression in art is also about exploring and comprehending what exactly one is feeling. With that self introspection and information, creativity can take shape and form in many ways and mediums. There's an old saying, that states when the going gets tough, the tough get going. Likewise, that is exactly what self preservation in creativity means to me.

Most definitely, there are limits within us, and even during fantastic times, it just may be difficult to create. May expounds on this a little further by saying, "Consciousness itself is born out the awareness of these limits. Human consciousness is the distinguishing feature of our existence; without limitations we would never have developed it" (May 114). Yet, he poses the question, "What if imagination and art are not frosting at all, but the fountainhead of human experience" (May 124). This gets me pondering more about my self preservation theory. I wonder if we are pushed to our limits, do we then become imaginative and create form in order to deal with such limitations? This was the question that I continued to challenge myself with as I refined my personal creative theory.

If one is to make a new future out of life not going as planned, I surmised and accepted as I had exposed to literature and lectures that if something isn't working, let it go. Let go of the past, and embrace your future. *When You Start to Let Go of Your Past, These 10 Things Will Happen,* is an article written by Dawn Hafner where she elaborates this point in more detail:

> When you keep replaying the past you are forfeiting your present. Once you decide to let go of the past, however, you become drawn towards new goals, new visions and new people that will lead you to an exciting fresh chapter of growth in your life. Our lives

our not meant to be static. Change does happen for a reason, and the less resistance you create against change, more growth is available for you. (Hafner)

Careful consideration of what needs to be shed, embraced and developed is also paramount. Along those lines, another image was constructed in the photo series (see fig. 44).

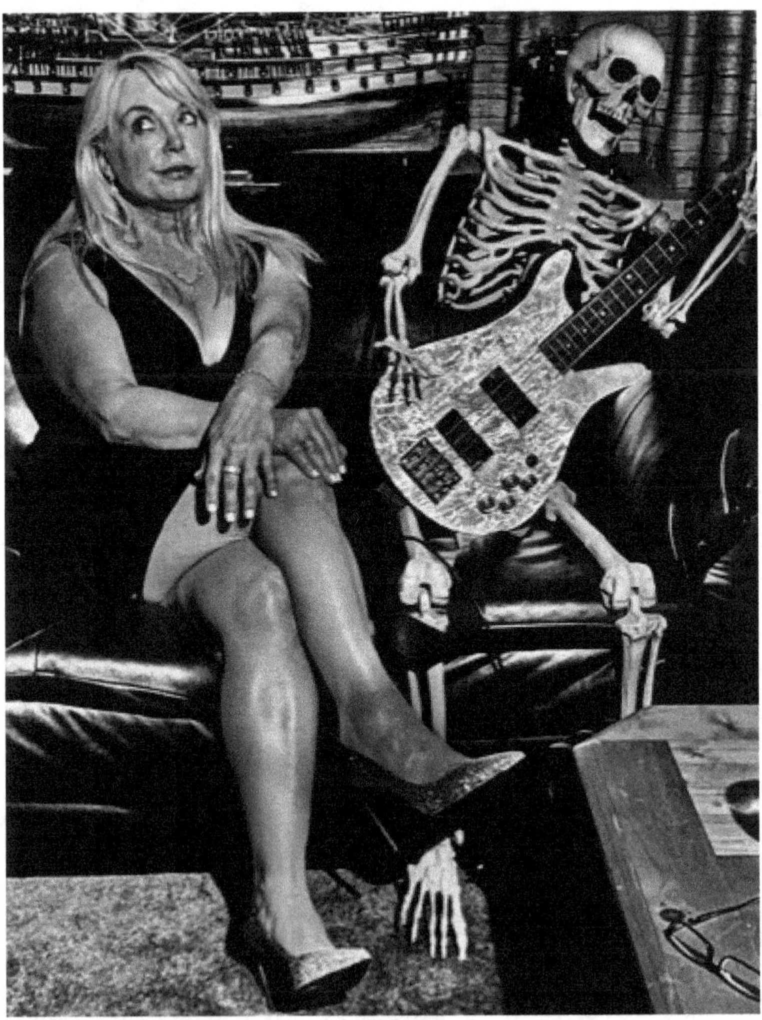

Fig. 44. Claudia Gray. *Same Old Tune*. 2021, collection of the artist.

In contemplation of the last few years, all the things I learned, endured and created, I started to think that in a way, I seemed to have made lemonade out of sour lemons, as the saying says. With taking a broader view of this timeline, all of the experiences are a part of my own life's journey. They might have been beautiful, hard, and painful, but they made me who I am today. Certainly, the last few years, as for most of the world trying to live in a COVID-19 pandemic, it has not been a comfy luxurious cruise. Rather, the trip ended up being on a very bumpy road on a rickety old stage coach.

Nonetheless, I continued to learn many life lessons, and created a thought-provoking photo series and finally possessed a personal creativity theory. Perhaps these years are one of the bad chapters in my life's book. Or perhaps this was the muck that the glorious water lilies are blooming out of and there's more flowers trying to bloom. Which reminds me of what Thich Nhat Hanh has often said, "No mud, no lotus." (Hahn). Either way, I self preserved and self expressed - true to my own creative theory. As Edward de Bono stated, "Creativity involves breaking out of established patterns in order to look at things in a different way" (Johnson).

In conclusion, I do not think that my creativity journey is over. After all, I hope to continue to live a happy, healthy and productive long life. So, now after much deliberation and contemplation on my past experiences, I know that I am a creative being. I can finally self-realize that perhaps I was even that way as a child. Although, not classically trained, I do have a need to produce form out of nothing.

I listen to inspiration and proceed to take to action. I may have my emotions and self expression come out in my creations. Or I may share Nature's bounty with the public through my photography. I may write to inspire and to decipher philosophies. I may paint while dancing in joy hoping someone will feel it as the artwork hangs in their home. I may make a piece of glass art, that was infused by good juju with Buddhist monks chanting in the background as I formed it. And perhaps someone will pick up the vibes, as I have often witnessed. I may even notice spirituality speaking to me through what I am creating, such as the dragonflies.

Currently, as COVID-19 is subsiding, the art world is waking up from hibernation. I have several art shows and gallery exhibitions already scheduled for my calendar. Additionally, I am happy to be curating more shows. I am also thrilled that I will be making presentations on my art and new photo series at various upcoming events.

Nonetheless, no matter what I know (and hope) my muses continue to keep busy with creating as life comes and goes. As with any community, I have come to accept that I am one of these crazy, fun-loving, expressive artsy people. More specifically, I am part of the creative flow, and creativity flows through me. I feel privileged, serene and happy finally really understanding and owning that creating is one of my life's purposes.  I am also so grateful that their is a profound wisdom that flows through me, and I am a mere channel for its purpose and message.

So along my creative expedition, I bid a sweet thank you to my mind for doing all its figured out and for what it is currently learning. I send a whole lot of gratitude to my ever-fun and very beloved Muses for all my past creations 'Til we meet again curious ones.

Until then, I can joyfully traverse life's ups and downs. Confident and secure that Mother Nature gives me vitality. Just like how I feel soaking in Yosemite Falls' energy, exclaiming, "I AM FREE!" (see fig. 45). Moreover, I feel REALLY alive and calmed, as I intuitively now know, I can express my creativity in one way or another. Through my journey, I have realized that in life, there is a beginning to every new beginning.

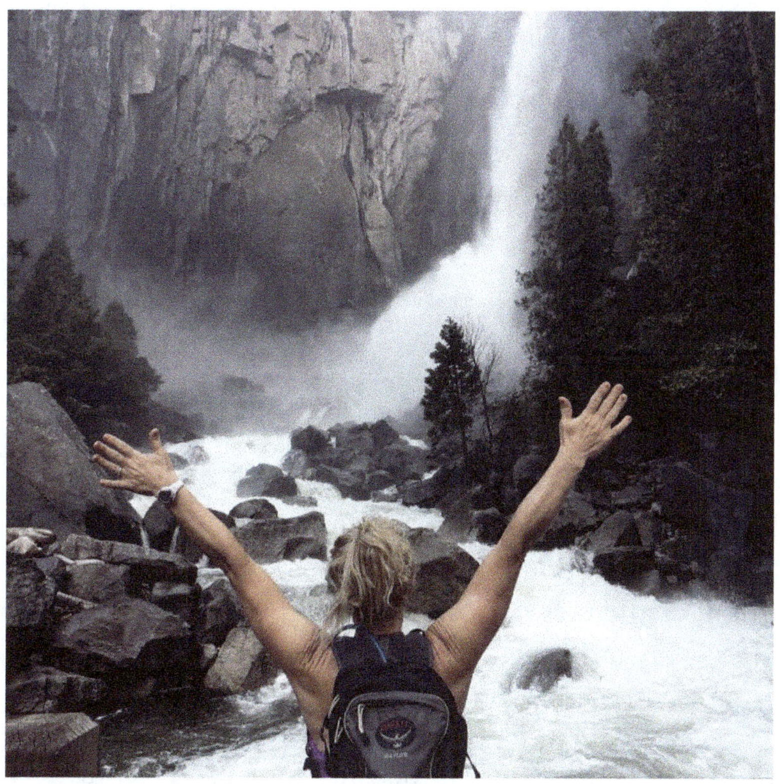

Fig. 45. One of my favorite all time things to do in nature is to raise my arms and shout "I AM FREE!" I shared this particular moment with my son, Tommy. I set up the parameters of the shot and Tommy captured this awesome moment at Yosemite Falls. Claudia Gray. *I AM FREE!*. 2017, collection of the artist.

# EPILOGUE

It has been a year since the completion of this manuscript and its publication. In that time, there were many personal turmoil challenges demanding my attention, and alongside many amazing synchronicities occurred. Logically there is no rhyme or reason other than I believe there is some spirit or energy behind its manifestation and guidance. Was it God, my Muses, or Universal Energy? It doesn't really matter as these are all subjective opinions of beliefs. However, I am most certainly aware of its existence in my life and artwork. I am also happy to report that my creative art journey continues to grow. After the completion of my graduate degree, I started to stretch myself as an artist and focus on my creative life and career. This past year, I participated in more art shows, gallery exhibits, Plein Air Painting groups, expanded my territories, reconnected with dear friends and revitalized my art networking.

In contemplating and dissecting creativity, for me, one thing is for sure, there does seem to be a wisdom that passes through the maker with inspirational purpose. My hope is that this book somehow gives you what you need to hop on your own transportation, start your journey and make some awesome creations in whatever medium speaks to you. Maybe you go slow, and go on a calm walk or stroll and start small. But whatever you do, seek your passion, live in it and create what you are supposed to create. It does not have to be pretty, or technically correct, just delight in the FLOW and PLAY that you may feel as time stops and you make something out of nothing. Wow… inhaling breath… and sitting with that concept in mind, I bid you safe travels my friend, and I hope our paths cross on our respective journeys.

# ABOUT THE ARTIST

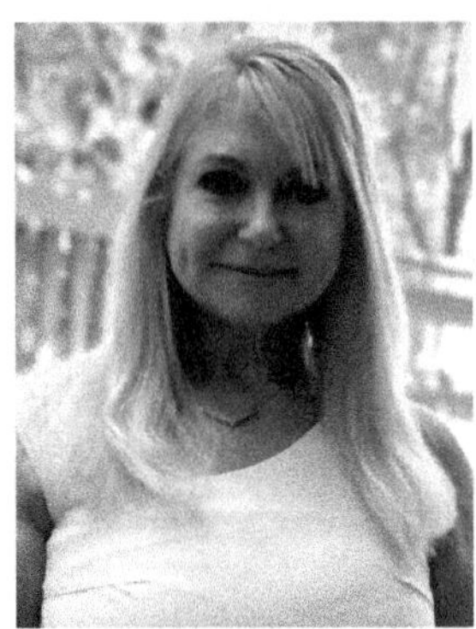

Fig. 46. Claudia Gray. *Vineyard Lane Self Portrait*. 2021, collection of the artist.

Claudia Gray, (aka Patricia M. Gray) is an award winning multi-medium artist, photographer, curator, author, and editor. She has exhibited in many galleries, museums, juried art shows, and her work is sold at various retail establishments.

Ms. Gray was an accomplished freelance writer and photographer, often wrote under the pen-name of Patricia M. Gray. Ms. Gray's photographs have appeared in many publications including the *San Jose Mercury News,* and national magazines. She has written for numerous high profile companies: national newsletters, such as, *HRBriefings*, the Trust for Public Land, California ReLeaf*'s California Trees*, the Santa Clara Valley Water District's *Aquacycles*, the Santa Clara County Library Reading Program, *E-Zine* for University of California Santa Cruz Extension, and many others. Additionally, Ms. Gray has authored four corporate OSHA safety manuals, and countless corporate policies and procedures. Ms. Gray's picture book manuscript, *More Please,* received an honorable mention award in a national writers' competition for the children's short story category.

Ms. Gray received her Masters in Humanities with Arts and Visual Media emphasis from Tiffin University. She graduated with honors from Loyola Marymount University with a Bachelors of Arts in psychology. Ms. Gray holds a Senior Professional in Human Resources (SPHR) designation, a Master Composter certification as well as a Wilderness First Responder certification. In the past, she was the book editor and a staff writer for the *Loma Prietan*, a Sierra Club newsletter, and held numerous leadership and civic roles. Ms. Gray volunteered teaching art at schools for eight years and currently serves on three Board of Director positions for a gallery, national women's art association, and a youth park organization. Ms. Gray's environmental efforts and art have been featured on FOX News, radio, newspapers and a TV show about her life and art. Most recently, she won a distinction award for her photo series, *A Woman's Work Is Never Done,* for her presentation at the Tiffin University Student Research Conference.

Ms. Gray cares deeply about the environment, is an avid hiker, backpacker, gardener, and life learner. When not creating art nor traveling, she enjoys tennis, golf, surfing, practicing Buddhism, and volunteering.

To learn more about Ms. Gray and her art journey, please visit www.graydesigns.org.

## WORKS CITED

"99 Inspiring Quotes about Art from Famous Artists." *ArtProMotivate.Com*, ArtProMotivate.com. Accessed 29 Mar. 2022.

Adams, Ansel. "Monolith, the Face of Half Dome, Yosemite National Park, California." 1927. *The Metropolitan Museum on Art, New York.*

Adams, Ansel, et al. *Yosemite and the High Sierra.* 1st ed., Canada, Ansel Adams, 1994. In-text citation

Adams, Ansel, and Mary Street Alinder. *Ansel Adams: An Autobiography.* New York, New York, Ansel Adams, 1996.
Andreasen, N. 2006. The Creative Brain: The Science of Genius. New York, NY: Plume.

Bagan, Barbara. "Aging: What's Art Got To Do With It?" *Today's Geriatric Medicine*, www.todaysgeriatricmedicine.com/news/ex_082809_03.shtml#%7E:text=Therapeutic%20art%20experiences%20can%20supply,pathways%20and%20thicker%2C%20stronger%20dendrites. Accessed 3 Apr. 2022.

Baobeid, Iman. "On the Importance of Names." *The University of British Columbia Equity and Inclusion Office*, students.ubc.ca/sites/students.ubc.ca/files/Importance_of_Names_Guide_v2.pdf. Accessed 30 Mar. 2022.

Bell, Clive. "Clive Bell : The Aesthetic Hypothesis." *Clive Bell : The Aesthetic Hypothesis*, facweb.furman.edu/

%7Edcummins/Clive%20Bell-%20Art.htm. Accessed 19 Mar. 2021.

Bellmer, Hans. *Die Puppe (The Doll)*. Gelatin silver print. Museo Reina Sofia, Spain. 1934.

Bergquist, Carlisle. "Comparative Theories of Creativity." *Vantage Quest*, 13 May 2013, www.vantagequest.org/treescomparative.htm#.YM5KbBNKhTY.

Callahan, Harry, et al. *Ansel Adams in Color*. 1st ed., Little, Brown, 1993.

Cavdarbasha, D. and Kurczek, J. "Connecting the Dots: Your Brain and Creativity." *Frontiers for Young Minds*, kids.frontiersin.org/articles/10.3389/frym.2017.00019. Accessed 25 Mar. 2022.

"Cindy Sherman - 310 Artworks, Bio & Shows on Artsy." *Artsy*, www.artsy.net/artist/cindy-sherman. Accessed 6 Feb. 2021.

"Cindy Sherman | MoMA." *The Museum of Modern Art*, www.moma.org/artists/5392. Accessed 2 Apr. 2022.

"Creativity | Definition, Types, Skills, and Facts." *Encyclopedia Britannica*,www.britannica.com/topic/creativity. Accessed 25 Mar. 2022.

Freeman, Michael. *Michael Freeman's Perfect Exposure: The Professional's Guide to Capturing Perfect Digital*

*Photographs.* 2nd ed., New York and London, Routledge, 2015.

"Georgia O'Keeffe | Artist Profile." *NMWA*, 29 May 2020, nmwa.org/art/artists/georgia-okeeffe.

Gill, N. C. "Can You Name All 9 Greek Muses?" *ThoughtCo*, 17 Mar. 2019, www.thoughtco.com/the-greek-muses-119788.

Gray, Alexandra. *Monet's Genuis: Musée de l'Orangerie*. 2019, author's private collection.

Gray, Claudia. *Bottle Display.* 2013, author's private collection.

Gray, Claudia. "Claudia Gray ~ Gray Designs." *Claudia Gray ~ Gray Designs*, www.graydesigns.org. Accessed 1 Apr. 2022.

Gray, Claudia. *Convention Booth. 2015*, author's private collection.

Gray, Claudia. *Candle Shop.* 2012, author's private collection.

Gray, Claudia. *Costa Rican Mist*. 2013, author's private collection.

Gray, Claudia. *Delusional Denial*. 2021, author's private collection.

Gray, Claudia. *Dragonfly Breaths*. 2017, author's private collection.

Gray, Claudia. *Dragonfly Ornaments.* 2015, author's private collection.

Gray, Claudia. *Dragonfly Sun Catcher.* 2015, author's private collection.

Gray, Claudia. *Endless Dust*. 2021, author's private collection.

Gray, Claudia. "Final Project Photo Series Movie Format Claudia Gray." *YouTube*, 8 Aug. 2021, www.youtube.com/watch?v=m1t6nxHNeaw.

Gray, Claudia. *First Show.* 2012, author's private collection.

Gray, Claudia. *Gallery Members Show*. 2021, author's private collection.

Gray, Claudia. *Glacier Point Photo Frenzy*, 2013 author's private collection.
Gray, Claudia. *Glass Wave Sculpture*. 2017, author's private collection.

Gray, Claudia. *Glimpse of Freedom*. 2019, author's private collection.

Gray, Claudia. *Honu.* 2015, author's private collection.

Gray, Claudia. *Horsetrail Falls.* 2013, author's private collection.

Gray, Claudia. *Horsetrail Falls Glow.* 2016, author's private collection.

Gray, Claudia. *Juried Photographs*. 2017, author's private collection.

Gray, Claudia. *Klimaschutz, Deutsche Studenten Protestieren*. 2019, author's private collection.

Gray, Claudia. *Madame Dragonfly*. 2016, author's private collection.

Gray, Claudia. *Marketing Brochure*. 2021, author's private collection.

Gray, Claudia. *Mixed Media Art Show*. 2021, author's private collection.

Gray, Claudia. *Molten Magma*. 2015, author's private collection.

Gray, Claudia. *Monet's Giverny*. 2018, author's private collection.

Gray, Claudia. *Mother's Day Surf*, 2019, author's private collection.

Gray, Claudia. *Orchid Tile Art*. 2012, author's private collection.

Gray, Claudia. *Pele Awakes*. 2015, author's private collection.

Gray, Claudia. *Red Dragonfly*. 2016, author's private collection.

Gray, Claudia. *Redwood Studio*. 2021, author's private collection..

Gray, Claudia. *Repose On Exhibition*. 2022, author's private collection.

Gray, Claudia. *Same Old Tune*. 2021, author's private collection.

Gray, Claudia. *Self Portrait: Happy Artist*. 2022, author's private collection.

Gray, Claudia. *Slumpy Etch*. 2012, author's private collection.

Gray, Claudia. *Surf Day*. 2019, author's private collection

Gray, Claudia. *Tea Set Candles*. 2012, author's private collection.

Gray, Claudia. *The Irony of Ironing*. 2021, author's private collection.

Gray, Claudia. *Vernal Double Rainbow*. 2017, author's private collection.

Gray, Claudia. *Vineyard Lane Self Portrait*. 2021, author's private collection.

Gray, Claudia. *Zambrosas*. 2019, author's private collection.

Gray, Olivia. *Cutting Glass*. 2015, author's private collection.

Gray, Claudia. *I AM FREE!*. 2017, author's private collection.

Hafner, Dawn. "When You Start to Let Go of Your Past, These 10 Things Will Happen." *Lifehack*, 25 Jan. 2021, www.lifehack.org/articles/communication/when-you-start-let-your-past-these-10-things-will-happen.html.

Hanh, Thich Nhat. No Mud, No Lotus: The Art of Transforming Suffering. Parallax Press, 2014.

"Hans Bellmer Artworks & Famous Photographs." *The Art Story*, www.theartstory.org/artist/bellmer-hans/artworks. Accessed 10 Nov. 2020. blatant objectification of women.

Harris, Elena. "Dragonfly Totem and Spirit Animal | Meaning." *Spirit Animal Info*, 10 Aug. 2021, www.spiritanimal.info/dragonfly-spirit-animal.

"How to Choose an Artist Name That's Google-Friendly." *DIY Musician*, 6 Jan. 2021, diymusician.cdbaby.com/music-career/choose-artist-name-wont-get-buried-bottom-search-results.

Indeed Editorial Team. "8 Ways To Find Your Passion." *Indeed Career Guide*, www.indeed.com/career-advice/career-development/how-to-find-your-passion. Accessed 1 Apr. 2022.

Johnson, Carla. "17 Famous Quotes on Creativity to Inspire Your Marketing." *Carla Johnson*, 18 Jan. 2021, www.carlajohnson.co/17-famous-quotes-creativity-inspire-marketing.

Libor, Jessica. "How to Practice Non-Attachment While Still Goal Setting in Your Art Career." *Medium*, 3 Mar. 2022, medium.com/the-visionary-artists-salon/how-to-practice-non-attachment-while-still-goal-setting-in-your-art-career-dcf9261c7cc1.
London, Barbara, et al. *Photography (Instructor's Review Copy). 9th, Upper Saddle* River, New Jersey, Pearson Prentice Hall, 2020.

May, Rollo. *The Courage To Create.* W.W. Norton & Company, 1975.

"Mindful Photography: The 4 Stage Seeing Practice." *Udemy*, www.udemy.com/course/mindful-photography-the-4-stage-seeing-practice/?utm_source=adwords&utm_medium=udemyads&utm_campaign=DSA_Catchall_la.EN_cc.US&utm_content=deal4584&utm_term=_._ag_95911180068_._ad_532194018659_._kw__._de_c_._dm__._pl__._ti_dsa-43646292608_._li_1014232_._pd__._&matchtype=&gclid=CjwKCAjwrqqSBhBbEiwAlQeqGoTeqG3BrjjGfl395BHE7B-u_MEzSxnjdDJHgdJDLTL7hw2WHWK6xoCk0UQAvD_BwE. Accessed 4 Apr. 2022.

"Mozi (Mo-Tzu) | Internet Encyclopedia of Philosophy." *Internet Encyclopedia of Philosophy*, iep.utm.edu/mozi. Accessed 31 Mar. 2021.

"Muse | Greek Mythology." *Encyclopedia Britannica*, www.britannica.com/topic/Muse-Greek-mythology. Accessed 7 Apr. 2022.

"Muse Quotes (336 Quotes)." *Goodreads*, www.goodreads.com/quotes/tag/muse. Accessed 30 Mar. 2022.

Museo Nacional Centro de Arte Reina Sofía. "Hans Bellmer - Die Puppe (The Doll)." *Museo Nacional Centro de Arte Reina Sofía*, www.museoreinasofia.es/en/collection/artwork/die-puppe-doll. Accessed 15 Apr. 2022.

Nickerson, Charlotte. "Emotional Contagion - Simply Psychology." *Simply Psychology*, www.simplypsychology.org/what-is-emotional-contagion.html. Accessed 26 Mar. 2022.

"Pele (U.S. National Park Service)." *National Park Service*, www.nps.gov/articles/pele.htm. Accessed 1 Apr. 2022.

Rosen, Marvin, and David Devries. *Photography & Digital Imaging*. 5th ed., Dubuque, Iowa, Kendall Hunt Pub Co, 2002.

Ryan, Kevin. "Hour of the Furnaces Edited Intro." *YouTube*, 2 July 2011, www.youtube.com/watchv=9_I5_oMrWYo&list=PLoiu4tcP04tgKl2N3gkr_9phiNDKr8SE7.

Sarinana, Joshua. "Photography and the Feelings of Others: From Mirroring Emotions to the Theory of Mind." *PetaPixel*, 26 Oct. 2014, petapixel.com/2014/10/25/photography-feelings-others-mirroring-emotions-theory-mind.

Silva, Jason. "What Is Creativity?" *YouTube*, uploaded by Jason Silva: Shots of Awe, 7 July 2015, www.youtube.com/watch?v=tYbA_-mAtUY.

Sontag, Susan. "The Aesthetics of Silence." *I Wish I Could Describe It You Better.* www.iwishicoulddescribeittoyoubetter.net/overseas/wp-content/uploads/2009/04/aesthetics-of-silence-sonntag3.pdf. Accessed 3 Feb. 2021.

Soriano, Caroline. "Why You Should Give Handmade Gifts When You Want To Make Someone Feel Extra Special -- Benefits Of Handmade Presents." *Sienna Likes To Party - Shop*, 29 Jan. 2020, www.siennalikestoparty.com/blogs/news/why-you-should-give-handmade-gifts.

Tate. "Community Art." *Tate*, www.tate.org.uk/art/art-terms/c/community-art. Accessed 15 Apr. 2022.

Tate. "The Art of Belonging." *Tate*, www.tate.org.uk/art/artworks/rothko-red-on-maroon-t01165/art-belonging. Accessed 26 Mar. 2022.
Thompson, Scarlet. "Claude Monet and His Water Lilies at the Musée de l'Orangerie." *Bridgeman Images*,blog.bridgemanimages.com/blog/monets-water-lillies-at-the-mus%C3%A9e-dlorangerie#%7E:text=He%20had%20a%20passion%20for,of%20 colours%20evoking%20different%20moods. Accessed 3 Apr. 2022.

"Three Big Changes in Three Years at HalemaÊ»umaÊ»u Crater (U.S. National Park Service)." *The National Park Service*, www.nps.gov/articles/000/three-changes-at-halemaumau.htm. Accessed 4 Apr. 2022.

Tolstoy, Lev, et al. *What Is Art?* Bristol Classical Press, 2011.

"Top 25 Passion For Art Quotes." *A-Z Quotes*, www.azquotes.com/quotes/topics/passion-for-art.html. Accessed 1 Apr. 2022.

Turnage, Robert. "Ansel Adams - The Role of the Artist in the Environmental Movement." *The Ansel Adams Gallery*, 5 Feb. 2020, www.anseladams.com/ansel-adams-the-role-of-the-artist-in-the-environmental-movement.

"What Is Public Art?" *Association for Public Art*, 4 Mar. 2021, www.associationforpublicart.org/what-is-public-art.

"What Is Slumping? | Bullseye." *Bullseye Glass Company*, www.bullseyeglass.com/what-is-slumping.html. Accessed 2 Apr. 2022.

Wikipedia contributors. "Claude Monet." *Wikipedia*, 1 Apr. 2022, en.wikipedia.org/wiki/Claude_Monet.

Wikipedia contributors. "Community Art." *Wikipedia*, 30 Mar. 2022, en.wikipedia.org/wiki/Community_art.

Zalmay, Kahar. "Why Festivals Are Important." *The News International*, 24 Feb. 2017, www.thenews.com.pk/print/188562-why-festivals-are-important.

www.ingramcontent.com/pod-product-compliance
Lightning Source LLC
LaVergne TN
LVHW050535100826
845148LV00002B/573